MW01633317

An Entrepreneur's Guide to Responsible Wealth

How to Build It, Enjoy It, and Protect It!

RESPONSIBLE WEALTH
AN ENTREPRENEUR'S GUIDE TO
RESPONSIBLE
WEALTH
How to Build It,
Enjoy It, and Protect It!

Published in the United States of America, by The Institute of Responsible Wealth
First edition

Book design: The Brand Artist, Inc. / www.thebrandartist.com

Library of Congress Cataloging-in-Publication Data
ISBN-13: 978-0-9817003-1-1
ISBN-10: 0-9817003-1-4
Congilose, Frank.
An Entrepreneur's Guide to Responsible Wealth / Frank Congilose

To my wife Diane,
for years of believing in me
with her continual love and support
in all that I do. Thank you for
allowing me to be me!

Preface

Financial freedom and security are terms that are often synonymous with wealth and success. With the recent uncertainty in the economy, the confidence that many individuals and businesses had in building financial freedom and security has been shaken and possibly altered forever. Because we are in extraordinary times, traditional methods of building wealth and security have changed. The collapse of a thriving real estate market, the neurotic stock market and failing financial institutions have changed the game for virtually everyone with assets and evaporated massive amounts of wealth. Unlike in the past, almost every asset class, whether equities, commodities or real estate, have declined and been set back. The amount of government intervention and bailouts to get the economy on track continues to build upon an already out-of-control federal deficit. As the government bails out financial institutions — and even the U.S. auto industry — it is clear that financial freedom and security have changed for many. The shining light in all of this chaos, however, appears to be the closely held and small-to-midsize businesses that provide quality products and services and can adjust as needed. These unique organizations continue to develop marketing plans and financial flexibility, enabling them to continue to thrive and succeed. As a result, the traditional mindset for building wealth by going to work for a large company and staying there until retirement is not what it used to be. The traditional strategy of working for the same company and getting that big pension or stock options does not necessarily have the benefits or security that it once had. The real opportunity for building long-term wealth and achieving financial freedom is in today's entrepreneur. In light of the opportunities that today's entrepreneur has, there are inherent risks. This is why today's entrepreneur needs to build *responsible wealth*, not wealth that is easily lost or confiscated due to taxes, poor planning or speculating in ineffective or unrelated business ventures.

For an entrepreneur, America truly is the land of opportunity, where people can find opportunities to achieve their dreams. Our history as a country is full of success, and the achievements of these individuals are part of our heritage. People come to America from all over the world to stake their claims and take advantage of the chance of living their dreams. The probability of success, and of sustaining this success, however, is not what you might think. In 2006 alone,

649,700 new small businesses emerged in the United States. In that same year, 564,900 went out of business and nearly 20,000 went bankrupt[1]. In all, about two-thirds of new employer firms survive at least two years, and only about 44 percent survive four years. And if that isn't enlightening enough, *family* businesses passed on to the second generation have only a 30 to 40 percent chance of keeping their doors open, and the survival rate sinks to 10 to 15 percent from the second to third generation. And the third to the fourth generation? About 1 percent survive!

Imagine spending your life's savings on a chance at success, or your life's work on something that barely has the probability of outlasting your grandchildren. Your time, energy, money, all gone, leaving no legacy. The day that you are not there is the day it all starts to crumble. Sometimes this is because there is no business succession plan. Or there may have been such an enormous tax bill that it robbed the business of its liquidity and left the next generation without the cash required to operate efficiently. We all know that the IRS does not wait for its money. Your heirs may be forced to liquidate the very core of the business that would have allowed it to continue. If you are going to put your whole life into becoming a successful entrepreneur, make sure it doesn't cost you everything.

Are you preparing properly? Are you formulating a succession plan with an exit strategy that provides you with the life you want and ensures that your life's work will build the legacy you want to create?

The good news is that you can truly build wealth, and have a life of happiness and success, if you do it the right way. You may still be at

---

1 http://www.sba.gov/advo/research/sb_econ2007.pdf; Table A.2 Business Turnover, 1985-2006, page 295 The Small Business Economy for Data Year 2006, A Report to the President, published 12/2007

the beginning stages, deciding if you want to be an entrepreneur, or you may be deep rooted, with a family history of entrepreneurship. Whatever the level of experience or exposure you have, there are several elements to consider. In my first book, *Discovering Responsible Wealth*, we discussed the individual's quest for financial security. Getting ahead of the curve can be a frustrating existence when the game board and rules are flawed at the onset. As time goes by, pieces are added and removed from the game, and all of the rules for winning keep changing. The business world is no different…*and* we still have to deal with all of our *personal* trials and tribulations.

The financial institutions themselves – banks, insurance companies, investment companies – will often make things harder for you and will always be a part of your life as a business owner. These entities are not necessarily on your side. They are for-profit, and derive income from fees and services. They sometimes unknowingly have agendas that, based upon profit, conflict with your agenda. Business owners want help, easy access to money and low interest rates. Conversely, the more money a bank lends with low interest rates, the less margin they retain, and the more it may hurt them. There is always a conflict, so the advice a business owner gets is rarely 100 percent pure. This puts business owners in a quandary. How do they know what to do when those who appear to be in support roles at financial institutions actually have conflicting agendas?

Building wealth and having a life of happiness also requires balance in areas besides finances. Being an entrepreneur does not have to come at the cost of everything else in your life. Most of us do not choose to lead lonely, unhealthy existences only to end up the richest person in the cemetery, but life for an entrepreneur gets so frenzied and complicated that we forget to maintain balance.

Should I Do It All on My Own?

No matter how much you fight it, things are getting more complicated and less efficient, and there is forever a challenge brewing. Terrorism, a real estate market downturn, a credit crunch…there is always a crisis, and there will always be a crisis. At the end of the day, there is tremendous pressure on a business owner. The people working for you and with you, as well as your clients, will put pressure on you from all sides.

You are an entrepreneur the day you open up your business, turn the key or give out your first business card. Once you have shifted gears, from that point forward every decision you make will determine your success or failure. Conversely, the absence of a decision will determine the same thing. Every decision that you make, at every moment, determines your future. Most people get so caught up in the daily noise of life that they lose focus on the moment. They cannot see the decision that is before them, and they begin spending time on unnecessary tasks. The next thing they know, their business is failing and they have no idea how it happened. Entrepreneurs become unconscious of what is actually occurring in the world right before their very eyes. Proper advice and coaching from qualified professionals that utilize a *responsible wealth* perspective will help guide you and make sure you are on the right track.

As an advisor, I can often walk into a business and tell right away whether it's succeeding or failing, just from what I see around me. I can sit in owners' offices and quickly ascertain what is going on based on the conversation. Are they building a business that has a life beyond them, or did they merely buy themselves a job?

Every entrepreneur needs an effective team that is astute and savvy in a variety of fields. One of my gifts is that I am very good at innovating. I can look at ideas from any industry and determine if those concepts are usable in my practice almost immediately, and I can see others' projects with the same clarity. It can be said that there are no new ideas. The same thoughts and ideas are just packaged differently. When we change the experience, products and services appear new and fresh again. Once, I gave a business idea to a friend, and he joked that he would only give me credit the first time he talked about it, but after that, it was his to keep! I was fine with that. When he used the concept, he reinvented the idea in his own way, making it his to claim.

The difference between success and failure is not about being lucky. There are certainly people who get lucky on occasion, but true success is about good, solid decisions. Because each of our perspectives is different, and each one of us comes from our unique set of circumstances, we might not even know what constitutes the *right* decision. We need a team of advisors who can present new ideas to expand our context and perhaps assist us in identifying golden opportunities we may have otherwise missed. Without our advisors, our limited context might stifle us.

If I wanted to learn to play golf, ideally, I would hire a professional or find someone who plays golf well to teach me how to play. My limited context of what I think a golf swing should look like may be vastly different from what a professional actually demonstrates. I would expect that the professional teaching me would demonstrate a swing, watch me replicate the swing and finally make suggestions for improvement. Finally, to perfect my game playing on the course, it would be ideal for my coach-professional to make corrections as we go along. If I want to make good financial decisions or good business decisions, I want to spend my time around people who are modeling those positive outcomes. These days, you can learn in so many ways. You can listen to a CD, read a book, learn online and the list goes on and on. There is no shortage of resources. Anyone you select as an advisor or mentor should also be a person who is aware of what is up-to-date, and someone who continues to constantly learn.

When choosing an advisor or a member of your team, you really need to select someone who "gets it." A very polished salesman or someone who is self-serving does not make a good team member or advisor. Don't be taken in because they have memorized the glossy brochure, or they dress in designer clothing and have the latest gadgets. If you took away the salesman's mutual fund, stock or insurance product and asked a real business question, would he be able to suggest a solution or opportunity for you? Again, a team member or advisor needs to be objective and put his or her self-interest on hold. An advisor, at least a *Responsible Wealth Advisor*, is a person who has a breadth of knowledge and experience from which to draw, and someone who puts you first. If you asked your current advisor a question and he or she was stammering for answers or serving his or her self-interest, how secure would you feel?

Be aware of egos that surface when professionals are vying for the job of advising the client. Often, control issues among advisors can emerge and they need to be resolved quickly. The various team members – from the financial advisor, to the accountant, to the banker and others – all want to be at the center of the wheel. Unfortunately, they may not be capable, let alone on the same page, or may even have hidden agendas.

My perspectives come from years of experience, during which I have assisted people in obtaining the right advice and making sound business decisions. I have succeeded as an entrepreneur by being both a business advisor and life coach to other entrepreneurs. Recently, a friend came to me struggling with whether or not to attend an evening business meeting. The meeting was more social in nature, and was not going to produce any additional revenue for his company. His alternative plans would have been to attend his son's baseball game. I gave him a bit of a challenging answer to help sway him. I said, "Well, I'm sure there won't be anymore business meetings, but there will certainly be lots more events for your kids!" His reaction was a look on his face which read: Oh, how could I be so ridiculous! The decision in the moment needs to be right, and you rarely get a second chance at life's lessons. Entrepreneurs have a responsibility to their business, but they also have one to their family and themselves. Success is having balance, not choosing optional business events at the expense of what really matters like family, health or faith.

I spend a great deal of time with my clients and associates. I know them personally, I know their businesses, and it is fair to say I know their needs, wants, wishes and dreams. Why? Because I *ask* them. Why do they listen to me? Because I also work at modeling the results they are looking to achieve. I am no better than they are, I simply have a process that I continually follow and a work ethic that is unwavering. I have taught myself to be in balance, and this little known secret is sometimes coveted by those who do not possess it. I choose to share my vision and strategies with as many people who will listen.

Your advisor needs to *be* an entrepreneur, or at least *think* like an entrepreneur. It is ideal when your advisor lives in the business world and also has a greater sense of what is occurring outside of the bubble. He needs to know about business, financing, protecting assets and how to transition assets for business succession planning, to name just a few requirements.

If an advisor is going to help you, you will be well-served if she adheres to the principles of a *Responsible Wealth Advisor*. This person needs to have a broad base of knowledge, and needs to know that there is more to life than just the bottom line. There is cause and effect for every decision that is made. This person needs to captain the team and possess enough leadership ability to facilitate change and progress. Overall, advisors need to listen to what your objectives are, not theirs.

Avoid choosing someone who is narrowly focused. Accountants, for instance, may be some of the best-educated advisors. Unfortunately, they are often unaware of what it means to be an entrepreneur. They know about P&L statements, compliance, and taxes, but sometimes they know very little about start-up ventures. They have a tough time breaking out of the perfect-world scenario and applying their skills to the real world of business. Yes, having a retirement plan would look perfect and provide a tax deduction, but if that money is required for cash flow or to build the business, sometimes it is better to take care of retirement later. Having the cash flow to survive and grow is the number one priority.

A *Responsible Wealth Advisor* looks at the total package. Financial responsibilities that are in your future – like college and retirement – will need to be funded. Advisors with a holistic view and perspective will enable you to fund what is necessary, but not at the expense of growing your business. They also understand that if you are a business owner who wants to grow, you will need to attract and retain key employees. For years, I have had the opportunity and pleasure to operate with this holistic view, and to teach other planners how to assist entrepreneurs and keep the greater good in perspective. I believe that, over time, these holistic planners, not the traditional planners or product salespeople, will enable today's entrepreneurs to get ahead. It is also important to recognize that many are trained to only help with individual planning needs, and are not necessarily properly educated or prepared in the intricacies of business planning.

It is my goal that this book serve as a guide to help you understand how to build the life you want as today's entrepreneur. Although I have provided some specific advice on the pages ahead, nothing can replace the value of a team of advisors who can provide you with the holistic guidance and insight to make your journey a successful one.

Chapter 1

Getting to the Top

The Investments You Make for the Life You Want

Most entrepreneurs are highly motivated by the pursuit of financial gain. They will work long, hard hours with confidence that their dedication will pay off in the long run. Initially, this reward will come in the form of financial freedom. And after the seeds have been sown, the reward will hopefully be in the freedom of time.

Despite the arduous years of business-building, people have a perception that entrepreneurs have either hit the career jackpot or were born into money with the proverbial silver spoons in their mouths. Often, a person's business ventures go unnoticed until many years have gone by and the business has flourished. Once the financial evidence of success is visible, others are envious. The sacrifices that a person has made to rise to the top, however, were probably too many to count. There is not a lot of glory on the way up the ladder.

In the recent presidential election, a small business owner ended up in the limelight when he expressed his concern over then-candidate Obama's stated desire to redistribute wealth in America. The entrepreneur known as Joe the Plumber made an excellent point when he said that he had worked hard and sacrificed to build his business. His concern was that it would not be fair to tax him more because his hard work had led to increased income. His comments reflected the belief of many entrepreneurs: Higher taxes dampen the desire to strive and succeed. As this incident illustrates, new initiatives will always surface, changing the game for the entrepreneur. Your ability to succeed will be a direct result of your ability to adapt and persevere.

Be prepared to have conviction in your decision and unwavering dedication in the pursuit of your goals and dreams for your mission of entrepreneurship, or you might not be prepared to give what it takes. The harsh reality is that many businesses fail. When you look one step further you will realize that we live in a country where we are failing in so many areas, not just business. We have a greater than 50 percent divorce rate, which leads me to believe that we are clearly having a difficult time balancing our personal lives. Take a look at the health crisis. The nightly news is full of stories about heart disease, cancer and other illnesses being a direct result of what we are doing to ourselves with poor eating habits and lack of exercise, some of which is due to a demanding schedule and a lack of time. And the problems go on and on.

What makes one person successful while another is not? Just as importantly, what makes one person stay on top while others fall off? Once the initial milestones are accomplished, staying at the top takes sacrifice, hard work and unwavering dedication. Who is truly winning the game for the long haul? What does it take – money? Many people believe that if they just throw enough money at something it will be successful, which is not true. It might just mean that you end up with less money! Does it simply take time? Do you repeat in your own head – *If I can just spend enough time at work, things will be fine*. Research tells us that entrepreneurs spend about double the amount of time at work versus those who work for someone else. Even though we have all heard the expression *work smarter not harder*, entrepreneurs can get caught in the trap of forgetting this sound advice. You might only find out that you have wasted a lot of your time if you are not generating more revenue as a result. The challenges that we have to endure (whether we create them ourselves or some other force manifests them into our world) can make us or break us.

Time

When you are an employee, you work for someone else. You arrive at 8 a.m. or 9 a.m., and you stay until 5 p.m. Once you leave the office, you typically do not have to think, worry or brainstorm about anything related to your job until the next day. The 5 p.m. whistle gets your mind racing about other things like making dinner, picking up your children, calling your mother or watching the Yankees on television. When you are an entrepreneur, your day never truly starts or ends. You wake up at 5 or 6 a.m. thinking about a project list or a bill that needs to be paid. And you worry at the end of the day that you may not have accomplished enough. There is no time when a business owner can punch out and not think (*or should I say worry?*) about things for the rest of the day. In many ways, owning a business is like having another child; you are constantly thinking about this "someone" in your life. However, with pain comes tremendous reward.

My golden advice to protect your time is this: Work when you say you're working and take off when you say you're off. If you can make the distinction between the two, it will take you a long way toward maintaining a reasonably balanced life and keeping your sanity. Go ahead and work long, hard hours because you need to when you are building a business, but be sure to stay focused and spend time on the things that are productive and that will pay off in the long run. There is a cost in everything we do. Most people can relate to a cost in terms of money, but the cost of time has even more value and may actually be significantly greater. Time is a gift. It is your greatest asset because no one is making any more of it, and you don't know how long you have. Have gratitude for the time that you have and do not waste it or take it for granted. Be in the habit of constantly reassessing how you are spending your time and determine if you are making intelligent choices.

While you are making an investment of time in your enterprise, your family and friends are making the same investment. If you are working 16 hours a day, your family has been without you for that same number of hours. When you look at the price you pay, don't just think of yourself. Keep in mind the price is often shared by every member of your immediate family and friends.

I have seen people use many excuses for allocating time in the way they do. They will spend lots of afternoons on the golf course schmoozing potential clients, and they will miss surprising their wife for a lunch without the kids on her birthday. They will not exercise regularly, using "not enough time" as an excuse, but will spend hours during a workday surfing the net. Make a mental note to ask if keeping yourself healthy rises to the top of the priority list of things for which you make time.

At times, entrepreneurs can get caught up in being important. We view our community standing as imperative for marketing our business and for our own self-worth. Although I am certainly an advocate for effective networking and involvement, our business and family time need to be just as important and really come first. Making a difference in our community, being a friend to our neighbors and participating in charities are vital, however, we need to do so on a balanced basis. Our time needs to be in check to maintain a happy and productive business *and* personal life.

Health

In the pursuit of your business, are you focusing your attention on the most important asset – you? Your health and well-being rely on mental and physical conditioning. Be a constant student of life and work at your personal development. Read books on the subject, or biographies of people who have made a difference in the world, or even consider listening to educational and motivational tapes when you are driving. Turn your car into a learning center. If you think you are missing entertainment by avoiding radio or TV, trust me, you are not missing much!

Are you taking care of your body? Have you come home from work at fifty only to find out that you need quadruple bypass surgery because you haven't exercised or paid attention to your diet in the last thirty years? There will be many costs of being in business, but one of them cannot be your health. Good health is part of a solid foundation—a building block— for a life of *Responsible Wealth*. Success in anything requires energy and focus, and your physical well-being should not be ignored or taken for granted. Having a good self-image and maintaining good health will also increase your confidence and help you overcome self-imposed limitations.

Stay current with your checkups with your physician and work with a qualified fitness professional. Do not make excuses about being too busy at work to fit this into your schedule. This will provide you with information regarding your vital signs and enable you to identify what type of nutritional regimen to use, and what physical activities and exercise programs would be appropriate. If you want to exercise, you should seek the advice and direction of qualified professionals in the area of physical fitness. The library, the Internet, local gyms and other resources are at your disposal for little or no cost to help get you started. You should monitor your exercise and measure your progress in order to be sure that you are accomplishing your objectives and using a balanced regimen. Many people have difficulty staying with a diet and exercise program, so working out with a partner and holding each other accountable in these areas may be very productive, while also making the experience more fun.

Mental and emotional development should receive the same attention as your physical health. "Garbage in, garbage out." Are you avoiding situations that are not healthy or are hindering your personal growth? Raise your awareness and make a conscious effort to improve those aspects of your life that need improving. Avoid activities and situations that may prevent you from reaching your objective, such as poor diet, consuming your time with excessive amounts of television, reading the tabloids, surfing the Internet or playing video games for hours on end in lieu of developing skills and abilities to help you grow personally. Many of these activities reduce our energy and hinder our ability to think and be creative without realizing it. We all require outlets which enable us to relax and find enjoyment. However, without proper balance we can stunt our personal growth by not spending enough time seeking knowledge and personal development. Television and video games are just not the real world and devoting excessive time to these activities does nothing to help you grow and develop. Don't passively watch others live out their dreams. Be active and live out your own dreams!

Family

When all is said and done, fulfilling relationships with people we love and care about are major aspects of life. Entrepreneurs often spend so much time building their business that they can be tempted to ease their consciences with their wallets. The guilt that can exist around your lack of time can put extreme pressure on you. You may even try to monetarily compensate your kids for the attention they have not received. The reality is that your kids would be better off if you taught them to think and know the right way to work, make decisions and strive forward in life. There is a golden opportunity in being your children's mentor – to teach them to work toward a greater purpose, not to seek immediate gratification. If age-appropriate, you might allow your child to work with you at your business to learn some of these lessons directly.

Spending money on children to overcompensate for what you have not done as a parent can have devastating effects on their personal development. Other people may envy this behavior from a distance. It is admirable that a person can provide such luxuries to his family. But when you get closer, you realize that some devastating effects may occur. Giving too much to your children prevents them from growing into self-assured adults. An entrepreneur strategizes, works hard, grows and succeeds. If you do not allow your children growing pains, they will have no achievements of their own to use as stepping stones. When you give your kids the car, spending money, vacations with friends and generally make their lives easy, you take away their struggle. You have forgotten that your own struggle is what got you where you are today. If you never had challenges in your life, you would have been unprepared to deal with adverse circumstances that might arise in business. Do not take away your child's ability to develop the backbone necessary to withstand life and its many challenges. A lifetime of *easy* teaches your children to be lazy. It does not allow you to transfer the principles that made you successful, and it robs them of a sense of accomplishment. We wonder why some of these children get addicted to alcohol, drugs or gambling!

I have always had agreements with my kids. When it came time for them to get a car, they knew well in advance that if they did their job – studying and getting good grades – that I would help them with what they wanted. I don't have to explain the appeal of having the freedom to come and go as you please! And, the compensation for good grades came with a variety of privileges. I believe that a person needs to be educated, so going to college was really not up for discussion. Helping them pay their tuition so that they would not go into adulthood with student loans was obviously an incentive for them to keep up their marks.

We have friendly negotiations about money, but none of my children have viewed me as their piggy bank. I have never acted like an ATM, so I never created any confusion that had to be unlearned. My children recognize how hard I work, and know that to be successful they will need to do the same. It was my job to *not* take that ability away from them. I have a twenty-three-year-old daughter who worked at my office for spending money while attending college. When she filed paperwork at my office, she was paid for that. Do a job, get paid. That's how the world works.

Being in business for yourself is difficult. Each day you are faced with challenges that need to be resolved, people who need your care, and tasks that need to be checked off the never-ending To Do list. And to add to the list of worries and concerns, being in business has risks. With risk comes stress, and with risk and stress comes the need to put in as much time as possible at the office. Balancing your time and family requires constant reassessment.

Put your mind at ease with this simple thought: The brass ring does not exist. As Wayne Dyer would say, "Success is a journey, not a destination." You really never do *arrive*. You just keep moving forward, because your alternative is quitting. Successful entrepreneurs typically do not quit or give up easily. They evaluate why something does not work, make changes and try again. Giving up and quitting is not an option. That does not mean that you won't stop to check if you have made progress. There will always be check-in times to make sure you are making prudent decisions. Your trusted advisor and team should always be there helping and guiding you along the way.

Financial

When you get into business initially, raising capital can create a number of challenges. You may find yourself borrowing money from your personal assets (or someone else's personal assets), or you may be personally guaranteeing a loan from a lender. There is often some element of risk in this, which inherently should lead to an upside of incredible reward. The downside may be devastating. The term OPM (Other People's Money), which we will explore, may be a viable option. Due to the risk-reward nature of entrepreneurism, every business owner needs to develop an ironclad protection plan, which I will discuss in detail in *Chapter 8: Protecting Real Assets.*

After you have fully protected yourself, the financial challenges that you face may at times feel infinite. Your business is likely to be your greatest investment of time and money and may be your greatest asset, but it is typically not a liquid asset. How do you invest your time, money and passion in something that you cannot even tap into? This creates major challenges for entrepreneurs in the early stages. Businesses go through cycles, and at certain times not only will you be using all of your extra time, but you may be required to invest additional capital as well. When you decide to reinvest your liquid assets into your illiquid one, it is imperative to look at the type of risk you are taking and manage the risk accordingly. What type of return on capital can you expect? What are you doing with the money? Should you invest in infrastructure, marketing or people? You need to continually pay attention to your return on capital. Unproductive capital needs to be converted to use as soon as possible. Hopefully, you have not created bad habits that are leaving you with little extra because you have invested all of your money in your lifestyle. As time goes on, this will certainly lead to problems due to the lack of capitalization.

Entrepreneurs are always *on*. They are always around their laptop, PDA, or cell phone. Don't expect that being a business owner buys you a rich lifestyle and a lot of free time. When you are in business for yourself life seldom gets easier, it will only change. If it is not some new federal regulation or compliance issue coming into your world and dictating new measures, it is banking reform tightening the noose on access to money. There is always a new challenge to address.

You will make many sacrifices in getting to the top and it is often a challenging journey. A business owner frequently gets squeezed on all sides. The lack of time creates constraints on your family life; it also leaves you feeling like there are not enough hours in the day to accomplish as much as you would like to in your business. And making time for yourself? Good luck! You had better get into good habits early on to eat right and exercise or you will be tempted to make excuses about your bad physique. Financially, you will struggle with where to find the money for building your business and how to best allocate resources. You and your family will constantly want a better lifestyle for all of this sacrifice, but financially you may not be able to accommodate everyone as fast as they may wish. And do not forget that the consumers and your employees will always want more for less. The pressure is on you, all day every day, to pursue that dream and purpose, and to build an organization that makes a difference. In spite of the challenges, the rewards for success are worth the effort. Are you ready to take on this wonderful, exciting, challenging career path called entrepreneurism?

RESPONSIBLE WEALTH SUMMARY

- *When a business is young, there is a trade off of time for financial freedom.*
- *You are the most important asset. It is essential that you keep yourself in good physical and mental health.*
- *Allow your children to earn their rewards in life. Do not overcompensate for your lack of time by indulging your children.*
- *Developing good habits for your time, health and finances will lead to great rewards.*

CHALLENGING THOUGHTS

- *Are you prepared to make the commitment of time and money that will be necessary to build your business?*
- *What habits are you fostering that will lead to success and a life balance?*
- *What steps are you taking to lead a healthy lifestyle of diet, exercise and personal growth?*

Chapter 2

Developing Your Goals, Vision & Purpose

Your Success Will Never Exceed Your Dreams, So Dream Big!

If we were going to watch a movie of our own lives three, five or ten years from now, what would we want that movie to look like? A good movie *moves* you. There are parts that make you laugh, cry and sit at the edge of your seat. The more talented the producer is, the more the movie affects you. Set your goals and aspirations with the same clarity and vividness. The more they *move* you, the more committed you become to those goals. The more you have a vision of how you want your life to manifest itself, the more you have a purpose. Purpose drives passion, and passion is what keeps you moving toward your goals.

In a typical week, I cannot see beyond the piles of client files on my desk or past the ten people constantly looking for help and information. It is like trying to stand up in a rough ocean with waves continually crashing on you – impossible. Every once in a while, you need to get out of the water and sit on the beach and look to see what is possible. Only then will you see the world differently. You need to dream. You need to dream big.

When I spend time envisioning what my life may look like years from now, only then am I working *on* my business not *in* my business. There is a difference. It is so important to have quiet time to use your mind like a giant whiteboard. Take time to reflect on how you would like your company to look in a perfect world, and think about how you personally would like to be living. Go through the process and write down what it looks like and feels like. Then, you can develop a plan to achieve your dream.

Some Questions to Help Guide You in Your Thinking:

- *How does it feel to be there, in the moment?*
- *What does each day look like?*
- *What do my relationships look like?*
- *How am I spending time with the people I love and care about?*
- *How do I spend time working on my personal development?*
- *Do I have time for myself each day to take care of my health?*
- *Do I exercise each day?*
- *Do I enjoy meals with my family?*

- *When I spend time with clients taking them out to lunch or dinner, am I eating healthy?*
- *Do I spend quality time with my family?*
- *Do I take vacations with my family and enjoy every day life?*
- *Is my spiritual life in the proper perspective?*
- *Do I pray or meditate every day?*
- *How do I live my faith?*
- *What does my personal life feel like as it integrates into my business life?*
- *How do I live financially? What is my lifestyle?*
- *What does the company look like?*
- *What type of facilities do we have?*
- *How is the business running?*
- *How are we doing with our business?*
- *Who are our customers?*
- *How did we get our customers?*
- *How do we service our customers?*
- *How do we market our product or service?*
- *How do we improve what we do from service to sales and marketing?*

Start by dreaming of the big picture, then come back to deciding how you are going to make it happen. Ask yourself: How does the rest of my life blend into the total picture? Don't limit your thinking because you have no idea what may occur! Put your ideas on paper, and suddenly they start to become clearer and more real. Goals can exist in many areas of your life. Let's think about someone in a romantic relationship. How do you feel when you are involved with someone? Are you happy? If you were to envision a life together with someone, are you communicating well? Do you have fun together? What type of activities do you enjoy doing? Are you going on vacations? How do you feel when all of these things are occurring? The more clearly you can visualize how you feel when you anticipate seeing this person, how you feel in the moment, and how the overall relationship feels, the more it becomes real, as you work every day toward making it happen and not being complacent.

For as long as I have been in business, I have always asked people if they have goals. Do you have a vision of what you are trying to accomplish? They always say, "Yes, of course!" The next question is, "Can you show me? Do you have your goals written down?" Suddenly, the answer changes from "Sure I do," to "Umm, not exactly." Or, for those who may have written them down at one point, when I ask them to talk about them, many can't even remember what the goals were because they have not looked at that piece of paper in such a long time. If you are committed to the things you want to accomplish, only then do you have a chance to make them happen. If you don't have goals that are written down, you will not remember them and therefore have no chance of achieving them. When you take time to focus on your vision and goals it is a concentrated effort. You are focusing on one particular thing, and your ability to focus is really going to determine your ability to succeed.

Sometimes I need to help people dig deeper in their goal development. If you told me that being in good health was extremely important to you, I would ask you "Why? How do you feel? Do you have energy? Do you take time for yourself every day when you are exercising?" Once I ask questions, I begin to help people capture *why* these things are really important to them and how they feel in the action of making them happen in their lives. It is when one knows those answers that goals become clear and attainable.

Communicate your ideas to others who are not dream stompers. Talk to those who will help you to be creative and who will support your end goal and enhance the idea. Don't be your own dream stomper either – it will sabotage your goals. If you envision yourself being fit and healthy, but visualize a double cheeseburger with all the toppings every time you pass a fast food joint, your goal is not clear. You are not committed to the goal of being healthy if what you are visualizing comes with a side of fries!

The more you put the goal out into the world, the more it gets clearer and you become more committed to it. When I first created the idea of the *Institute of Responsible Wealth*, I shared my thoughts first with my family and my close confidantes, then with some colleagues outside of my immediate business, and next with my best clients and other advisors. I wanted to gauge how my clients would receive the idea, and I even test marketed certain elements before moving full steam ahead. I communicated my ideas and the message and what I stand for, and what I wish to share with others. I received such positive feedback on how needed my message is in the world of finance that I realized I was on to something. You have to start building the dream. It starts with the entrepreneur, but you do not live in a vacuum. So use the talented, forward-thinking people in your circle to morph your ideas.

A word of caution on selecting your team: Its members need to be trustworthy so you never need to fear anyone stealing your intellectual capital. You may even consider putting a privacy (or nondisclosure) agreement together for them to sign in advance. This can be very cost-effective and quickly done by an attorney.

When I just started out in business, I had no idea what the possibilities were. Think of it this way...if you went outside on a cold day, you would breathe into the air and see your breath in front of you. Once the mist dissipates, your breath is still there but you cannot see it (although many think it has simply vanished). It is hard for people to understand what is possible because they are often dealing from a very limited context. I was in sales when I first went into business for myself. I still joke with my mother to this day because I knew she was asking, "Couldn't you get a real job?" She did not understand the world of sales and was viewing my career choice as a default for the lack of a real job. She would never say that today seeing my success, but the whole idea of being in business for one's self used to give the impression that a person could not get a job anywhere else; if you cannot be employed, you had better be *self*-employed.

Interestingly, very few people who succeed in sales started out with that intention. Something often happened and they just ended up in sales. Then, when they became successful, they often ventured toward entrepreneurship. If they could promote someone else's business, they could certainly promote their own! Let's say a salesman of an equipment company did all the bidding to local general contractors. As he learned the business and met all of the key players, he realized the areas in which he could do the job better and more efficiently. And let's face it, even when working conditions are good, people working for someone else generally lack the freedom to do things the way they would like to see them done. So, logically, a good salesman begins to think about starting his own company.

Once you start thinking outside of the norm, opportunities present themselves. I started my financial practice by taking my clients through traditional planning. One day my friend Earl had a huge impact on me when he showed me a totally different vantage point from which to approach planning. I realized that I was able to take what I already knew about my industry and customize my own process to benefit my clients.

Seeing your purpose, your vision, or your future does not always start out as an epiphany; it is not always grand. But you might have heard that a dream without a plan is merely a wish, so get working on your plan! Maybe you start by building a successful company that makes it through the week, month or the year. Then you begin to have the time and focus to start laying out a broader plan of what is possible. What do you want your business to look like three years from now? Be careful not to analyze the details or think too hard about how to implement your ideas at the beginning of the brainstorming stage. Getting into the *how to* too early may hinder your thought process and limit your thinking. After you have exhausted your brainstorming, it is time to begin the process of prioritizing and develop a plan. Once you create a plan and start delving into the details, the final stage is implementation, which is what will enable your ideas and dreams to become a reality.

Goal Diffusion

In 2007, my younger daughter was fortunate enough to play softball for a team that made it to the Babe Ruth Softball World Series. The tournament was held in Eagle Pass, Texas – a place that I had never heard of until that time. Upon careful review of where we were heading, I discovered that it is located in the southwest corner of the state, just outside Mexico. Because of my scheduling issues, my wife and younger daughter went to Eagle Pass before the tournament, while my older daughter and I followed a couple of days later. My initial reaction to being in the southwest corner of Texas was that I had never seen such large ranches. They seemed to go on for miles on-end. We found the people who hosted the tournament to be some of the nicest people we had ever encountered. I remember that, when I got there, I saw a sign that read *Where Yee-Hah meets Olé* – which gives you a taste of the culture. Going into the tournament, the girls were all very talented and focused, ready for anything that may have come their way. As the tournament went on, however, the heat, exhaustion and some dissension took the girls out of their game and they went from being the first seed in the primary rounds to getting knocked out early in the finals. The problem was *goal diffusion*.

Goal diffusion is the inability to maintain your focus on achieving your goals and objectives. It allows other distractions to prevent you from accomplishing what you want. For many people, goal diffusion occurs without them knowing it. This occurs not because the goal is impossible, but the commitment to the end-result is unclear or the person has not fully committed to it. It happens in many aspects of life, not just in business. Interestingly on my return trip from Eagle Pass, my older daughter and I left early because I was scheduled to attend the wedding of a close friend's daughter. Not totally focused on the road signs, I inadvertently missed a turn. After driving for almost an hour, it occurred to me that something was not right. Everything looked the same – large ranches that went on for miles – but the compass in the car said I was heading south. It finally occurred to me that we had missed a turn and were going in the wrong direction. We had to retrace our steps to get back on track. Fortunately, our flight was delayed, so we still made it. The moral to the story, however, is that every road looks like the right road when you don't know where you are going. The faster you realize where you are and where you want to be, the faster you get what you want.

If you do not have a clear goal or purpose, deciding how to spend your time will become very challenging. The less clear the goal, the more likely *goal diffusion* will set in. Here's how it works: If you are trying to build a business and you also like golf, the minute someone calls you and invites you to play a round, you will be off to the golf course. If you really are not committed to growing and building your business, you will be distracted by something that is more interesting in the moment. It is no different than choosing to take one more appointment with a client instead of supporting your child by watching his playoff baseball game. You really were not fully committed to the goal of being present for your child. Like my cousin Marco would always say, "*Diff*usion equals *con*fusion."

In order to build a successful life, you need to have a single, clear vision, or you will not be able to resist the distractions that arise when any diffusion enters your life. Even challenges are more easily overcome when the goal is clear and you are committed to your objectives. Many of us agree to do everything we are asked because we want to be nice to everyone. We end up volunteering for too many things and spend time away from the things that are important to us. This is why having clarity and a balanced life is essential. Having relationships with your kids is not diffusion from your business goals. The balance helps you decide what to say *yes* to and what to say *no* to, and helps you identify the right decision to make at the moment, in order to get the future that you want.

When Tiger Woods is lining up his shot, do you think he is wondering, *What's for lunch?* Or, *I really need to call about that landscaping for my backyard.* Or, do you think his mind is completely clear and focused on the shot? Tiger has already envisioned taking his shot and the ball going into the cup long before he swings his club. He has played out the entire hole and knows exactly what he wants to accomplish, without any distraction. If you are not focused on your own shot in life when other distractions are coming at you, you are going to hit the shot poorly.

When professional athletes are in the zone, they are phenomenal. However, after they lose their purpose in their sport, their lack of balance becomes abundantly clear. According to Ken Ruettgers, an NFL alumni who started a support website called GamesOver.org, many NFL players end up bankrupt, divorced or unemployed just two years (after retirement)[2]. A few of the top ten challenges of transition listed in the website are: lack of significance and purpose, divorce, substance abuse, financial loss, feelings of anger, bitterness, jealousy and depression. I would guess that many of the challenges they face are a direct result of the lack of purpose they now feel. If any of us were to focus our entire life on one element, we would be devastated with the void created by its loss. And what do people naturally want to do with a void? Fill it with something else – drugs, gambling, carousing,

---

2 Ken Reutters. www.gamesover.com

alcohol and so on. People who need to fill a void surround themselves with people and things that make them feel good only in the moment, which inevitably leads to bad decisions.

Do not consider investing even one dollar in being in business if you do not have a clear vision and clear goals. You will end up doing things just for the sake of doing them. Just like in bumper cars, you will go from bouncing off one car to bumping off the side rails. In the bumper cars of life, some people are wandering around in an unconscious way. They are surviving life on auto pilot, not living it.

If you are an entrepreneur without a purpose or vision and with plenty of goal diffusion, you will make poor choices and look like a ship that has been blown off course. Years ago, my friend Tim said to me, "Frank, you make money in your business. You lose money in everybody else's business." He was trying to encourage me to focus my efforts in my own business and not try to get rich by investing in businesses in which I have no experience. Otherwise, you're like the dog that's always chasing cars – he never catches them, and he is always out of breath.

"Fake It Till You Make It" is Not a Good Strategy

A sure-fire way to create misaligned goals is to allow your ego to control your life. Leave your ego out of it. I tell people all the time, "Do not try to keep up with the Joneses. Chances are, the Joneses are broke." One of the fastest ways to suffer from goal diffusion occurs when you are more preoccupied with making your BMW payments than you are with getting your company off the ground. Ego, in the financial world, does nothing but cost you money. In this case, your image will backfire when you least expect it to. Clients notice your extravagance and cannot help but wonder how much they are contributing to your new toys. As the Bible says, "He who humbles himself will be exalted, and he who exalts himself will be humbled." It is a myth that you need to fool people into thinking you are successful. The book *The Millionaire Next Door*[3] tells us that millionaires are not out there wearing their money on their sleeves. Success is not defined by what you are trying to show off, it is defined by the quality of life that you are living and what contribution you are making to others.

Live beneath your means. If you earn $100,000 per year, live on $80,000. Every business has a cycle and unless you are preparing for the down years, you may not have the staying power to keep your business open. You might be operating your business to the best of your ability, but if your customers are not doing well financially they will not be able to use your services for a time. Do not spend future money today because that is a quick way to bankrupt yourself and your business. The most successful entrepreneurs do not carry much personal debt and very little to no consumer debt (credit cards).

Opportunity vs. Entitlement: Worlds Apart

No one will ever wave a magic wand and say "*Voila*! You get everything you want in life!" If you grew up in a house where you did get everything you ever wanted, you may not have had the chance to enjoy life because you never had to work for your rewards. Therefore, your sense of accomplishment may not have matured.

There are those who live in the World of Opportunity, and those who live in the World of Entitlement. If you look to create

---

3 Thomas J. Stanley, Ph.D. and William D. Danko, Ph.D. The Millionaire Next Door (New York, Simon & Schuster, Inc. 1996

opportunities, have a vision of where you want to go, choose to move forward, and you take responsibility for where you want to be in life, then you probably live in the World of Opportunity. If you are fixated on the idea of others doing things for you – wanting to take lots of time off, wanting to be paid more for the same work at the expense of others, asking customers to buy from you even though you are not providing value – then you likely exist in the World of Entitlement. The World of Opportunity may require you to work hard, but in this world you have control of your destiny, which will ultimately let you earn control of your time and money.

If you are living in The World of Entitlement, you may soon notice that people start distancing themselves from you. They will likely grow sick of hearing you complain. If you think it is someone else's job to take care of you, you are giving up control of your life. If you hire people from this world, be prepared to be plagued with problems. Some want high salaries, all the bells and whistles of a great healthcare package, and lots of time off in exchange for as minimal work as possible. They have not earned the right to want anything, but they feel they deserve it just for showing up for work each day.

If you want control of your life, you have to take responsibility, and that is the only path to being fulfilled. Building a life of opportunity and a life of *ResponsibleWealth* puts you in the driver's seat and in control of your destiny.

Do What You Do Best

I met with a business owner one day who confided in me that his business was off the mark substantially and that his cash flow was suffering. So I asked him for his thoughts on what he might do to help improve the situation. His response was that he needed to go out and spend more time with his existing customers and concentrate on developing new relationships. Naturally, I asked why he wasn't already doing those things. He responded that he had been taking care of payroll issues and that he had lost some administrative staff, so he was covering those responsibilities. Effectively, he was taking his time away from what was crucial to his survival.

This happens to many of us. Even though we know we cannot be all things to all people, in the very early stages of business we do not have enough money to pay someone to do all of the tasks that need to be accomplished. In the beginning, business people need to be jacks-of-all-trades. They need to spend the time and effort it takes to get the business moving forward. Later on, they should be able to hire part-time, contracted people and/or consultants to build the team slowly so they don't have to do all of the work.

My son has a new band and they are starting to make a name for themselves. They are still managing every piece of their experience. They make their own flyers, call the clubs looking for gigs, hand out tickets to their shows and move every piece of equipment before they ever go on stage to perform.

This is the way many of us manage our new businesses. We pitch our products, then run the vacuum and open the mail in our offices, hoping that in a year or two we will have the funds to hire people to help us. As you start to succeed, you must force yourself to do this – it is the only way your business will ever grow. If you continue to be bogged down with tasks that are not making you money and are eating up your time, you will be using your most vital resource – YOU – inefficiently! If your time is worth $100 an hour, and you are doing

$8-an-hour work, you are not fostering the life you want to live. If you fast forward to my son's band experience, in a year from now someone else should be in charge of everything other than the performing. The faster you can streamline the tasks of your business so that you can just sing your song, the faster you will be successful.

My success as a financial advisor came when I had someone else scheduling my appointments, completing applications for financial products, inputting information into the computer, cleaning my office on the weekends, and opening the mail. Once I could spend the majority of my time in front of associates and clients, I saw exponential growth in my income and time. Suddenly I went from doing everything to only doing the things that I do best. By giving up control and letting go, you will even empower others to learn and achieve a better life. The last thing you want to be as an entrepreneur is a micromanager because it will stunt your growth. And if you feel that you absolutely cannot let go, chances are you have hired the wrong people. If I am worried that my phone is not being answered properly, I am going to reach for it every time it rings. If I am worried that my paperwork is not being completed thoroughly, I am going to spend time reviewing and proofreading everything. Once someone assumes ownership for what they are trying to accomplish because you have shared your vision with them, you are able to free up your time and spend it where it is most valuable.

When I started my financial services practice, I was able to slowly build my business. Because I had a clear vision of what I wanted to manifest, I knew who I needed to ultimately hire. Have the vision, support it, communicate it to others, then use your unique abilities to leverage the growth of your business.

How Far Are You Willing To Go?

What is it that you really want and what would make you happy? Why is it important to you? What are you willing to do to get there? Are you willing to pay the price for what you want? Do you have a clear goal and purpose and do you possess the commitment and passion to stick with it? If it requires additional knowledge, experience and education, are you willing to spend the extra time putting your plan together and to make the necessary investment? Are you committed to putting the right team of people together? Have you made the decision to spend time with people who are successful and happy, and not with people who feel helpless and entitled? Begin talking to other entrepreneurs and people who are already successful. You will find that, not only did they do the work to get there, but they are proud of their success and feel a sense of accomplishment and gratitude.

If you want to be a good parent, spend time with people who enjoy parenting and have been successful raising and communicating with their children. Ask them about their life as a family. Do they get together for meals? Do they share details about their day? How do they live their daily lives? My mother has strong, old-fashioned convictions, and to her, family is everything. Even now, we all get together for dinner on Sunday nights. We were raised to believe that everything revolves around family.

If you are interested in knowing more about your faith and gratitude, find people who are connected spiritually. Maybe they seem at peace and in tune with their faith. Ask them how they got to that place. How does that person live her faith? Probing can at times open you up to insight that you never knew existed and offer a perspective that may change how you view the world.

Many people travel through life without noticing what is really going on. They are completely unaware about what they are thinking. They are the conscious-unconscious. When people are in this mode, they are just reacting to life and going through the motions. They are the ones who, at work, are running around in circles collecting a paycheck and making no contribution. These folks cannot wait until the end of the week so they can cash their checks. They think that all they need to do is show up, and when they go home they fill the void again with sleeping, television, Internet, drinking and so on. There are only twenty-four hours in a day. Some people accomplish greatness. Others just breathe in the air.

If you take the day for granted, suddenly it is tomorrow and you are doing nothing again. Why is someone saying TGIF all day on a Friday when their only plan for the weekend is to sleep it away? That can get pretty boring. When you open the door on a Monday morning, it should not feel like the movie Groundhog Day, with each day monotonously repeating itself. You need to constantly reevaluate how you are creating value for others and reassessing if you are living on purpose. Then you need to create value and work on how you communicate it to your customers. That clear vision will always help you stay focused and will provide fulfillment as you accomplish your goals.

Your Integrity & The Platinum Rule

How you feel about your business, how you follow through and how you treat people help define and express who you are, your level of integrity and your purpose in life. You walk the path of your true intentions every day, and others are a witness to your actions. Let's say you are at a restaurant and the waitress mistakenly undercharges you by $20. If you realize the mistake and acknowledge it to your associate, you have a choice to point it out, thus maintaining your integrity. Otherwise, you will be taking advantage of the error that will likely cost the waitress money, and your associate's view of you will forever be damaged.

Living your integrity happens at every minute of every day. You are always living your purpose. If you look at life that way it is very easy to make good or wise choices. Lots of authors and business people have reiterated the phrase, *There is no right way to do the wrong thing*. This message pertains to your business as well as your personal life and if you are inconsistent in one or the other, an imbalance is occurring. *The decisions you make in the moment determine your future, and the easy decision is not always the right decision.* Sometimes you have to rise to the occasion and maintain your level of honor, even when it is inconvenient.

When you make the choice to make business a long-term proposition and not a get-rich-quick scheme, you do not want to risk losing your freedom as a means to an end. Making a decision that is illegal or unethical may be a quicker solution, but cheating others will have consequences. Even the college student who cheats on exams or takes shortcuts on projects may go on to graduate, but getting a degree versus getting an education can have life-long implications. I would rather my children get an education than a degree. In business, I would rather gain a client than make a sale.

Do not cut corners at the expense of your integrity or your relationship with others. Your job is to enhance the life of those around you – that is your purpose. The golden rule is to treat others the way you would like to be treated. But I believe in the *Platinum Rule*: Treat others the way they *want* to be treated. When you raise the standard higher, you create a business opportunity that will attract others.

Stewardship – One Step Further

Many people think that the word stewardship means donating money, or that it is a reference to the church. Although the connotation is at times for religious purposes, I am using the word in a broader sense in this book. Whenever you are trying to positively impact the lives of others, stewardship will come through. Being an entrepreneur is a form of stewardship. Treating people with integrity, keeping your word, doing the best with your money, or keeping the environment clean are all forms of stewardship. Stewardship should come through in all aspects of your life. It is about understanding that everything is a gift, and it is your purpose to share your gifts with others. It is your obligation to do things to the best of your ability.

Clients and friends sometimes ask how I blend my faith into my everyday business life. If you realize that you are here on this earth for others, you will do everything to the best of your ability. If you are clear in your mission and you work to the best of your ability, you will find that those who work for you will act accordingly also. If your staff is not following your direction, it may be time to reeducate them or hire people to be properly aligned with the values of your organization.

On Retirement

I have noticed that people who have a true sense of purpose do not talk about retiring. I heard Sophia Loren comment in an interview that retirement was such a sad word. What she was effectively saying was, *Why would I want to retire?* Her purpose is doing what she loves, performing. Why would she ever need or want to give that up? Why would anyone want to retire from creating value for others? Why would you want to stop having a purpose? Over time, you might change how you spend your time, but the notion of retirement is an odd concept to me. Do I simply stop working and play more golf? Sooner or later my golf game will fade and become boring. I am constantly looking to improve on all of the components of my life that bring balance – my life's work, my relationships, living my faith and creating value for others.

Entrepreneurs have chosen their fields because they want the opportunity to make a difference. They want to be their own bosses, to make a difference in the world and propel it forward. Being retired often means less income, loss of identity, and sometimes a loss of purpose. The opportunity to create value, stay engaged and earn income can be much more enjoyable if you find something you really enjoy and can use to make a difference. You might decide to never retire.

Overall, I would guess that most people lack goals, purpose and vision. When you tell certain people that you *do* have them, they think you are a dreamer. And when they laugh at you, what they really mean is: Why don't you act more like me? Misery does not just love company...misery loves *miserable* company even more. Surround yourself with people who recognize that life is an opportunity, who know how to use their talents and who want to expand them. For those people, the challenges of life are just inconveniences because their purpose continues to propel them forward.

Your vision must encapsulate your entire life. When you look long-term at the entire package, always be able to identify the greater purpose in what you do. Once you lose your purpose and stop creating value, you start filling the void by seeking solutions outside of yourself. People go to their doctors looking for quick fixes with medication that they see on TV commercials. Pharmaceutical companies offer pills for everything, each with a list of side-effects that are worse than your original symptom! In everything that you do, there is cause and effect.

The clearer you are about what you want, the sooner the idea moves from thought to paper, from paper to sharing, and from sharing to action and commitment. Sharing your vision with others helps you to be even more committed because your family, friends and associates will continue to ask about your projects and inspire you to live out your dreams. The more often I say something out-loud to others, the more they will follow up and support me in where I want to go.

When I started out in the financial service field, I was out giving advice to individuals and business owners. Then I decided to teach others how to be advisors and I went on to grow an entire organization. The purpose of the *Institute of Responsible Wealth* is to teach an entire culture to take responsibility for its finances. Twenty-five years ago I didn't have the vision to change the world. My vision, and yours too, evolves as we grow. Get out of the water, sit on the beach and think of what is possible. Do not limit your thinking. It may not be clear today, but as time goes on it gets more in focus. You might be ahead of the curve, and as the old adage goes: When the student is ready the teacher will appear. Life's experiences appear and occur at the right time. You can't really write the script of life anyway because God is in charge. If you believe that already, you understand what I mean.

RESPONSIBLE WEALTH SUMMARY

- *Take time to work on your business, not just in your business.*
- *Spend time envisioning what your life will look like years from now. Ask yourself questions that will help you visualize how things will look and feel.*
- *Communicate your ideas to people who will support you, who are positive, and who are trustworthy.*
- *Keeping focused and having clear goals will reduce goal diffusion.*

CHALLENGING THOUGHTS

- *Have you taken the necessary time to consider how you want your life to look?*
- *What goals have you formulated that you are working to achieve?*
- *Do you live in the World of Opportunity or in the World of Entitlement? How are you adding more of the right people and experiences to your life?*
- *Are you willing to put the time and effort into building the life you want, or have you been looking for a quick fix? What action steps have you taken?*

Chapter 3

Wealth Building Blocks

The Importance of Keeping the Balance

For most people, success is relative to the circumstances of your life at this moment. Our perception tends to be that we need more of what we already have in order to be successful. Hardly any of us feel that we have *arrived*. If we have plenty of income, we might be striving to increase our net worth. If we are at a healthy weight, we might still wish to incorporate better food into our diets. If we are content with our existing love relationship, the way to maintain interest is to continually look for opportunities to share new ideas and interests. As the saying goes, *If you aren't growing, you are dying on the vine.* Another way to say it is, *If you're green you're growing and if you're ripe you're rotting.* I believe that our desire to have more and be better is part of what makes us successful entrepreneurs. We never allow ourselves to kick back and watch life pass us by.

I believe there are five Wealth Building Blocks, or critical aspects of life, that we need to focus on to be ultimately happy and to build *responsible wealth*. I define *successful* as having a sense of peace and contentment. They are as follows:

- *Spiritual Life*
- *Physical & Mental Health*
- *Relationships*
- *Career*
- *Finance*

You probably noticed that finance is last on the list. I certainly recognize that money makes many things possible, and I believe wholeheartedly that it is important. However, the other four areas add significant wealth to our lives and need to be incorporated into the balance. Try to envision your life as an orchestra. You are the conductor and you get to play the music that makes you happy. Each aspect of your life is an instrument that makes a contribution to the symphony. When every instrument is playing on tempo, your life is in harmony. The music is a blessing for everyone around you. With this analogy in mind, recognize that life requires a delicate balance of time and energies. *As ye sow so ye reap*. That's why achieving a balance among faith, health, relationships, career and finances is critical to long-term success and happiness. If any one of these aspects is neglected, it will ultimately affect the other aspects of your life. If one of the instruments is offbeat, the music is out of sync. Imagine if several instruments were out of tune or missing a beat at the same time – you would hardly recognize the music and it would probably give you a headache.

Spiritual Life/Faith

For many of us, the exercise of identifying our goals, dreams, and vision takes tremendous soul-searching. Each of our lives has a purpose, and it is not always easy to identify it quickly. Some figure it out early, and others take years to identify it and move forward, if they ever do. Let's say that you are meant to be an entrepreneur, and you choose to move forward in that direction and pursue your dreams. As in any aspect of your life you will have challenges and difficult times. These are the times in your life when faith comes into play. Your faith will ultimately be what carries you through the tough times. If you have never read the poem *Footprints in the Sand* by Mary Stevenson, I would encourage you to do so. Lack of faith and a balanced spiritual life will often provide unnecessary worry, anxiety and ultimately diffusion. Diffusion and worry will always prevent you from living the life you want and finding inner peace.

Do you have a spiritual life now? What is it that you believe to be true? Are you living your life in a consistent manner with your beliefs? Do you spend quiet time each day on prayer and meditation? There have been many difficult times for me in my life, personally and professionally. I have noticed that during these times I am studying the scriptures and relying on my faith to pull me through, and it has never let me down. Faith provides inner strength and a positive outlook, whereas lack of faith leaves you fearful and weak. My faith does not always make my immediate wish come true, but I am always comforted by inner peace and clarity for my next step of life.

Accept the perspective that God loves you and wants the best for you, and that you were put on this earth for a purpose, and be happy about that! Have an attitude of gratitude and appreciate every day as a gift and an opportunity. Show your thanks by giving back to your neighbor in all that you do – including your business endeavors. Have a purpose for your entrepreneurship that makes the world a better place. Pray for the ability to make wise decisions and to be surrounded by others who will help you by providing their strength and insight. As my good friend Dave always says, "Live your faith. The answer will come." Having a foundation in faith will make the hard times less worrisome, which will keep you from losing your balance.

Physical & Mental Health

As we will find, and we will discuss this more throughout our time together, you are your best asset. If you are your best asset, you want to take care of yourself. If you understand the statement that *your body is your temple*, you have to ask yourself a few questions. Are you treating it right, or are you polluting it with toxic waste? Do you go to the gym? Do you eat fruits and vegetables? Do you maintain a healthy weight?

Like inner spiritual peace, good health is another building block that needs to be kept in balance. If you spend the first half of your life trading your health for your wealth, you may find yourself spending the rest of it trading your wealth for your health. If you want to be there for everyone around you and for your business, you need to fire on all cylinders. If your engine is in disrepair, or your tank is empty, you will not be productive because you will not have the energy that you need. Life is difficult, and you need all the elements that are within your control to be in check, and this includes your health. The more discipline you have for eating right and exercising, the easier it is to withstand life's challenges.

Your mental health is also vital to this delicate balancing act. If you are not saying positive things to your inner self each day, the negativity will consume you. If your business, relationships, health or finances are not what you want them to be, consider if any of this could be due to the barrage of counterproductive thoughts you keep putting in your head. *Garbage in, garbage out*. Practice activities that increase your positive outlook on life like exercise, spending time with loved ones, or participating in a charity. Do not constantly focus on elements that take your energy away like drinking, eating junk food, reading the tabloids, or conversing with small-minded people. Be careful of the media, too. Watch how others around you react to the news reports on the state of the economy. People often react to what they hear, and create a self-fulfilling prophecy. If you take on negativity, it weighs on you. Imagine that each unhealthy thought is a rock that you pick up and have to carry. Each time you pick up a rock, you put it in your backpack. Over time, your pack becomes heavy and onerous, and you feel as if you are carrying the weight of the world on your shoulders. Having balanced mental health involves shedding the burden of excess baggage and concentrating on holding onto the positive elements that will fuel your success.

All of us need some down time every now and then to recharge our batteries. We all need to decompress and spend at least a small portion of the day doing something unrelated to work. In these times you may want to surf the Internet, read books for pleasure, play golf, or go sailing. As part of good mental health, you need time away from your work to clear your mind; just be sure that you do not let your extracurricular activities take over your time. When things are in balance, it is fine to incorporate some fun into your life. When things overall are not in balance, you will find that you are not accomplishing the elements that are vital to your success.

The better you treat your mind and body, the happier you will be. With happiness and contentment comes success. You are what you believe.

Relationships

You cannot like or love others if you do not like or love yourself. It all starts with you. On many levels, our life is a mirror of what is happening inside us, so if you do not have a healthy relationship with your spouse, children, co-workers, or others, you probably have some work to do from the inside out. Bad relationships can be a clue that you are not attracting positive people into your world, or that you are putting your own negativity into situations.

In order to have a good friend, be a good friend. Treat others with kindness, respect, and be there for them when they need you – whether they ask or not. Spend time around positive people because they will encourage you to stay on the right track. Be forgiving of others, too. Your friends and family will not always do things the way you want, but the reality is that you will not do things exactly the way they want either. Due to our sum total of experiences and simply who God designed us to be, we are all different.

Walk the walk for your kids. Be the role model that you want them to have; don't wait for someone else to take the lead. Just because your spouse may have more time available for them does not mean that your role is not crucial to their development. Your kids need both of their parents, not just one. Also, building a lifelong relationship takes years. Do not expect to show up when they are all grown-up to find your "buddy" waiting for you. Relationships are earned, not given.

Live in the present with the people in your world; do not spend lots of time delving into the past. The past is the past. If the aftermath of yesterday is still affecting today, fix it. Be quick to apologize for a mistake that you might have made. Solve problems by working through them and then move on with your life. None of us knows how much time we are going to be given, so do not waste the precious moments with old nonsense.

Be a good listener and constantly improve your communication skills. The ability to really communicate with others is invaluable. It will see you through tough times and hard negotiations, and help you be there for your loved ones when they need it most. Show your openness and do not show judgment. You cannot judge others until you have walked a mile in their shoes.

And lastly, having relationship balance will largely come from the trust that you have with your partner. If you don't have trust in your relationship, it is very difficult for an entrepreneur to be successful and happy. This is not a nine-to-five job. Many business owners work long hours, entertain clients at night, or take business trips. If your spouse does not trust you, or does not trust that your actions are in the best interest of your business and family, it will become overwhelming to battle this on a regular basis. Part of any business is your relationships with others. If you are out fishing or golfing with clients all day, your spouse might not perceive that as work. If he or she is constantly hovering over you with a magnifying glass, inspecting your every action, life will become stressful. When I hire new associates in my business, I have a detailed conversation about spouses. I ask them if it will cause a problem if they are not home for dinner. I also encourage them to think about whether they have had a relationship up until this point that has been trustworthy, one in which they have not given their spouse a reason not to trust them. To be a successful entrepreneur, you need to have a very high level of integrity and honesty all the time. There is no room for anyone to doubt you, so don't give them a reason to.

I have seen people fail in business because their spouses just never got comfortable understanding that it is not a "normal" job with a "normal" paycheck. For those who have a difficult time balancing their relationship with their spouse and their personal finances, this can be especially stressful. If your spouse has a tendency to worry about money, you might choose to keep some of the financial details to yourself early on in business when finances are tight. There is no need to create unnecessary worry for the other person, assuming that you are not making poor decisions and putting your family in harm's way. If your spouse does understand money, and is in the endeavor with you, this might be a tremendous support system for you. Unfortunately, this does not always exist.

Because of busy schedules, it was easier for me and more practical for my wife not to be heavily involved in my business. We have found what roles work best in our family, and she has had enough on her plate taking care of the house and our three children. As Bill Cosby once said, "I've seen that job, and I don't want that job!" I make sure that

I do not micromanage her activities in the house. Just as I know what is going on at the office, she knows what is happening in our home much better than I do. There is a lot of multi-tasking and emergency management. My wife has allowed me to concentrate on my business, and I have allowed her to run the business of our household. You've heard the saying, *A happy wife is a happy life*. Incidentally, there are services that provide a family office to those who can afford to hire out some of the household duties. If you are having a challenging time in your relationship because there is an overall lack of time for these duties, this might be a solution for you. A person will make sure that phone calls are made as necessary, bills are paid, laborers are hired when needed, and other types of personal duties are completed. For years, the very wealthy have hired people to perform these duties, but now it is becoming more mainstream for high-income earners. In many families, the spouse takes on all of that responsibility, in addition to handling everything for the children, and it's not like the old days! Your kids don't grab a bat and a ball and play outside with their friends all day long. Sports are highly organized, and played in distant towns. They require separate uniforms, and there is a lot of expensive equipment. All of that requires coordinating and arranging, not to mention a lot of driving.

No matter which relationship is at-hand, all relationships take trust, communication, and a mutual give and take. As an entrepreneur, you have the chance to be a leader and set a positive example in all areas of your life – work, home, with co-workers, with your kids and so on. Keeping balance to have healthy, happy relationships is an essential building block in enjoying a life of true wealth.

Career

As an entrepreneur, you will do well and like certain aspects of your career. You may do other things adequately, but you may not like them and they might not be the most productive use of your time. For long-term happiness and success, you need to develop a process for how you conduct business and build your organization. We all have certain talents and abilities that make us unique. Dan Sullivan has explored this area extensively through his program *Strategic Coach*. Ideally, entrepreneurs should leverage their time by spending it in the areas where they are most productive. Many times, other people will identify abilities in you that you do not know you have, so do not hesitate to ask your close confidantes for their opinions on the areas in which you excel. Essentially, when you can harness your unique ability and the value that you create for others, it will take you to places you never thought possible.

One of the unique abilities of any business owner is that you are the one who can create the vision. What is the experience that you are offering? The type of business you have is immaterial. If you do not know anything about marketing but you have a coffee shop that has great coffee, you had better hire a marketing person to spread the news. Whenever possible, delegate and build a support team of other experts around you. If there is no capital to hire someone for a particular job, go to the Internet, read books and learn how to get your message out there. If you have a vision, spend your time in your most productive areas. If you allow yourself to be distracted by other things, your business will be less productive.

Being happy with your career path provides yet another fundamental building block for success. Find your passion and execute it! Work hard. When you create value, you become an asset to others and that provides both organizational and career security that everyone is really looking for.

Finance

My first book, *Discovering Responsible Wealth*, primarily concentrated on the Wealth Building Block of Finance. What do you want to accomplish financially, and why is it important? We are all responsible for how we use our money. Do you have a healthy balance of spending money on charity, wealth enjoyment, and wealth accumulation? All three are important.

Have you planned for the possibility that your earned income could change or be diminished by something out of your control, like illness or a lawsuit? Are you aware that lawsuits happen even to good people? As an entrepreneur, you must protect your business and money with an appropriate legal structure and adequate insurances. Responsible people act responsibly. Have you prepared a business succession plan or developed an effective transition and retirement strategy? There will come a day in all of our lives where we may want to scale back or change our work life either due to choice or necessity. If and when that happens, are you educating yourself on the effects of taxes, inflation and succession?

The Financial Wealth Building Block is one that cannot be underestimated. Whether we like it or not, money is the mechanism by which we judge success. That is not because money is important. What money can allow you to *do* is important. Financial freedom can help you enjoy a better quality of life. Having it can allow you to give to a charity you wish to help. Having it can allow you to help your children get their dreams off the ground or help someone who needs assistance. Having it can help you get well if you become sick. The benefits are limitless.

As I learned from one of my mentors, Dan Taylor, the name of the game is progress, not perfection. No one will ever be perfect or will be able to expertly juggle his/her life flawlessly. There is a lot of give and take that happens, but just being aware of what it is that you are looking to accomplish is the key. Last week I was not feeling well and I had a very hectic schedule. I noticed that I was eating much more than normal and was feeling the effects. Instead of obsessing about my failure, I added an extra half-mile to my daily running. I feel much better this week and the extra laps have given me some increased energy during the day. Becoming obsessed with balance will be counterproductive, but recognizing its value will bring so much joy to your life. From Monday to Friday afternoon, I work nearly around the clock. However when Friday comes around, my family knows that I am there with them all weekend. And when I say I am there with them, I mean in spirit, not just in body. And this means ditching my cell phone, too, which can really sabotage time and attention these days.

Your ability to multitask can help you with balance also. I have found that driving in my car to and from work or appointments makes great time to catch up or check in with clients, friends and acquaintances. I have a lifelong friend, Steve, who I love to call from the road and check in. Recently, when the granddaughter of one of my clients had surgery, it was a perfect opportunity to call him on the way into the office. I find it very efficient to combine the activities of my life. When I run in the mornings, I use this time for prayer and meditation. One never takes away from the other; in fact, I find that each enhances the other experience.

Not everyone is designed to be an entrepreneur, and not every entrepreneur balances life the way they need to. If you do not possess the ability to manage a new element in your life that is going to command much of your attention, while also remaining balanced in the five Wealth Building Blocks, perhaps you have some soul- searching to do. If you are a superstar in your business and you are making a lot of money, but you are dropping the ball everywhere else in your life, you and those around you will probably not be happy or satisfied. Achieving balance is the pinnacle of success. But again, this is not a game of perfection, it is something for which to strive.

> *"I am careful not to confuse excellence with perfection. Excellence, I can reach for; perfection is God's business."*
>
> *- Michael J. Fox*

RESPONSIBLE WEALTH SUMMARY

- *Maintaining a healthy balance in life is critical to success and happiness. You are only as strong as your weakest link.*
- *There are five Wealth Building Blocks – Spiritual Life, Physical and Mental Health, Relationships, Career and Finance. Each one plays a role in the wealth of your life.*
- *In striving for a balanced life, the goal should be progress, not perfection.*

CHALLENGING THOUGHTS

- *In what ways do you attempt to grow in each Wealth Building Block?*
- *Are you leading a life that is consistent with your beliefs? How are you modeling your faith to others? Do you see evidence that you are building important relationships in your life?*
- *Do you have a healthy relationship with money by allocating money for charity, wealth enjoyment, and also wealth accumulation?*

Chapter 4

Increasing Your Top Line

The Client Experience Determines the Top Line

In order for any business to be successful, it needs to create value for someone else. Not everyone has the talent to manifest this concept, however. It takes a special person to be in charge, and a great leader can communicate his vision in a way that others will follow. People want to share in your dream so they can be part of something larger than themselves. When you look at a business, no matter what size the entity, even the clients and customers come along for the ride when they believe in the brand and know what the leader stands for. Everyone involved is vital to the process.

When we look at why one company is successful and another is not, it often starts with having the right person at the top. If the owner ended up in charge by default, he merely has a job that he happens to own. The management style in that scenario tends to be very dictatorial. A business like that will rarely grow and will typically not succeed very long. That type of atmosphere breeds disgruntled employees and unsatisfied customers. Unless the process or business itself was so unique that it could stand alone, it will ultimately come down to the quality of leadership, which starts with the entrepreneur himself.

Every business has different products and services and the idea is, of course, that there is a market for your concept. Your platform must be different or better than that of someone else. Regardless of your competition, you differentiate yourself with the experience that you create. From the moment the first customer walks through the door or calls on the phone, the experience begins.

Have you ever walked into a business where you were dismissed the minute you walked in? You can picture it, I'm sure. You walk up to the front desk where a cranky employee hands you some forms to fill out and tells you to take a seat. If you had the opportunity to teleport yourself to another office, store or shop, you would be out of there in a heartbeat. What does *your* front office say to your customer? Does the first person who interacts with your clients exude care and concern for the job, or is this person chatting with co-workers about weekend plans while ignoring a valuable asset – your customer?

The person who answers the phone or greets the customer needs to make the customer feel welcome and happy to be there. It doesn't matter if the business is a lumber yard or a boutique, how a person is treated and her overall experience is what will ultimately make or break a great business idea. Having a professional environment does not mean that everyone is in a suit and tie; it simply means that they are creating the personality that you want your company to have. I get compliments all the time on the woman who runs my front desk. She remembers people's names, and she is warm and inviting to our clients.

Years ago, I went to look for a new car. A small foreign manufacturer had just entered the market, and I was interested in what they had to offer. I went to a dealer's lot and looked at a certain popular sports car. I was dressed in a suit because I had just left an appointment with a client and the salesman approached me. He said, "Can I help you?" and I responded, "I'm just looking." In all these years, I have never forgotten his reply to me. "You can't just look. You have to deal or you have to leave." In twenty years, I have never even looked at another car by this company. One person in a small dealership tainted my entire view of a brand. Is it fair? No. Is it reality? Yes.

I have car dealers today who actually call me and bring a car right to my office to test drive. They pick up my existing car for servicing, and they will come to my house if need be. It is all about the experience, which has kept me tremendously loyal over the years. That other company never even got a second chance with me. My last several cars have been purchased through a company that I am loyal to because when I need anything they are there. They make me feel comfortable about spending my money with them. Even after my service appointments, I always receive a follow up phone call. That's the *right* experience.

After you have welcomed your clients with open arms and treated them respectfully, you also need to follow up. Do what you say you are going to do. I hardly go a few weeks without someone mentioning that a contractor came to their home for an estimate, and then they never heard from them again. My personal experience in writing this book reaffirmed that poor follow-through exists in many industries. I had lunch with a team of publishers one Friday afternoon. The two gentlemen were professional and we had a successful meeting. One month later, I finally heard back from them. Too bad for them I had already chosen to work with someone else. Had they been in touch sooner, they would have gotten the business.

Clients do not want to feel as though you are too busy to handle their business or deal with their needs. Part of the experience that you have revolves around how you are treated, and the feeling of knowing that someone wants and values your business. Sometimes it is extremely clear why one business succeeds and another one fails. Picture walking into a restaurant where the hostess is friendly, you are seated in a reasonable amount of time and someone greets you and takes your drink order right away. That is why a business succeeds. Let's say you had the opposite experience. You walk into another restaurant where the food is equally good and slightly less expensive. However, you wait seemingly forever to be seated, your waiter is in a bad mood and it takes ten minutes to get your drinks. Thinking through this exercise, you realize that the price does not matter all that much. You feel good going to a place where you are valued. You feel frustrated and disheartened spending money at a place that does not care about you.

I have a client who is a very successful physician. When we last met, he could only see me at 7:30 a.m., and when I arrived he already had four people in his waiting room. I found out that his office typically has a two- to three-hour wait. This cannot be a good experience for his patients or their patience! It doesn't matter what industry you are in, the client remembers the experience. Did you feel terrific when the interaction was over or did you feel disheartened? I know a contractor whose specialty is swimming pools. He jokes that in his profession, it's a love-hate-love relationship with the client. When you first meet the customer, they love you. They are filled with anticipation about their new pool and they value the experience they are getting from him. Next comes the hatred they feel because the process of having a backyard in shambles disrupts their life! Then, when the project is over, they love you again. It is really no different in any business: give the clients what they want. Follow up throughout the process. Always treat them with respect. If they continue to love you, you have done a good job. If you delivered the experience and you have really "WOWed" them, they will even refer you to others!

The wrong experience sometimes revolves around being sold something that you do not need or want. My daughter brought her SUV to her college in Connecticut. The car broke down while she was up there, so she brought the car to the local dealer – not the person from whom we bought the car. They gave her every story in the book about how she likely had a faulty service job, needed a new battery and so on. She was getting more upset as the cost was going up and up. After asking her a few questions about the problems I said, "Where did you last get gas?" If you have ever had a bad tank of gas, you know that can wreak havoc on a car. I called my original dealership's service manager to confer with him, and he agreed that I might be right. So he called the service people in Connecticut. At the end of the day, they flushed the gas lines and all was well with the vehicle. The experience was such a negative one that my daughter would never consider using them, and she warned her friends at school not to use them either.

When you or your team deal with clients, never talk down to them. Businesses get into trouble when they start forgetting that they are in business because people *can't* do everything on their own. Customers are intelligent – they just aren't experts in your field – if they were, they would not need you! Talk to your consumers as equals. If I go to my doctor and have a question, I need to feel comfortable enough to talk it through. If the communication is broken, I will most likely not be a satisfied patient. The same goes with someone walking into your bike shop. If a woman is training for her first triathlon and does not know what type of bike suits her, she wants help. What she does not want is your teenage helper scoffing at her inexperience.

Common sense is not always common. You might think that everyone is doing these things well, but I can tell you from my experience as a consumer and a business advisor that this could not be any further from the truth. In fact, over the years I have seen an overall decline in the customer experience.

Delivering the right experience builds trust and loyalty. But remember that you want your customers to come back and to refer you to their family, friends, and acquaintances. Businesses can only grow when they have more people using their services. You want fans! You want people to talk about what you provide and tell others about you on a regular basis.

Getting Commoditized

When you enter a market, you are not the only game in town – and if you are, it's not for long. As time goes on, competition emerges. A fitness club in my area is a great example of this situation. Years ago, there was one club in my area. Everyone in town was excited when it opened, but as time went on their equipment started to get rundown, the facility seemed worn, and it was not as clean as it had been in the early days. The staff was complacent because they had no pressure to improve the situation. About a year after the downward spiral began, another club opened about a mile away, and it was busy very quickly. Look out, here comes competition! If the original center could not have differentiated itself from this new one, sooner or later all of the clients would have defected and gone elsewhere.

Commoditization is a process that reduces a marketplace to price competition. If the value of your business is lost there is nothing left to differentiate one product or service from another except price. I always laugh when I see commercials for insurance that boast "No salesman will call you."That is a clear indication that they do not value the person who would be providing that service. They are bluntly admitting that the consumer base has had such bad experience with insurance salespeople in the past that the company has decided they will simply be the cheapest game in town for the moment.

When service and a good experience are not there, it's all about price. I probably do not have to tell you that when it is all about price, you are very close to being out of business. You can only operate for so long without a margin. And the opposite is true too: people will pay a whole lot more for a valuable experience. People are willing to spend five or six dollars at Starbucks in a hurry, even though they can buy a cup of coffee just about anywhere nowadays. The draw is how people feel being in Starbucks. They are treated nicely, someone makes their coffee just like they like it, there are velvet sofas and the list goes on. However, when you arrive at the drive-thru of another coffee chain, the experience is much different. It's still coffee, but the delivery method is significantly different. Ultimately, whether we are selecting food, beverages, a doctor or an estimate for new electrical work, our decision criteria pretty much comes down to how we feel about our experience.

The laws have changed in financial services over the past few years. There used to be boundaries prohibiting one type of financial business crossing over into another sector and offering other types of financial products and services. For example, banks were not permitted to offer life insurance and investment companies could not do banking. Today, there has been significant deregulation, and they are all in each others' business. Consumers are starting to wonder whether the objective opinions they used to get from their accountants, for example, are still unbiased. Clients can read the shingle: CPA & FINANCIAL SERVICES. The doubt sets in. Are they still being objective? Is this right for me or is this product or service being proposed because this person is making money on the sale? Suddenly, commoditization is in the air. Clients may feel as though they are paying too much money for something, which forces the prices down.

The United States has been known as a service economy for many years. Much of our manufacturing has been lost to areas of the world where production is infinitely cheaper, so we have replaced revenue from widgets with revenue from services. Interestingly enough, we are now seeing a significant shift of labor for our services to places like

India and the Philippines. So now, even the service work is not being performed here in the U.S. Major accounting firms even have clients' 1040s completed out of the country for a fraction of the cost. If that service can be contracted out, the risk of commoditization is upon us. Unless you deliver a better experience, there is no need for you.

We would all pay a little more for a good restaurant. Given a choice in any industry, I believe that people will pay for the service that stands out from the pack. Whether it is your electrician, plumber, doctor, lawyer, favorite coffee shop or even hair salon, the top line of a business is driven by the feeling that a person has when they go through your company's experience. You cannot necessarily change the products that you have – perhaps there is little that you can do to even improve them – but you have full control over the experience. People are more inclined to think less about the product itself when the overall experience is positive. When every one of your employees conveys the same experience to the customer, you will build your brand.

Building A Winning Team

If you understand that people are your greatest asset, you know that having the right people in the right positions is vital to growth and success. Hiring the right people will allow you to focus on the things that *you* do well to continue to grow the business. When the right people and managers are around you, they are able to handle all the other areas, and when people are doing what they do well, they are engaged and happy to bring the right experience to your customers. This fosters the right culture and a brand that will be easily identified by the customer.

Final Thoughts

When you are creating your vision early on, part of your mindset needs to focus directly on your customers receiving a value-added experience. After you have brainstormed during your own quiet time, consider interviewing your existing clients for their perspective. What would the perfect experience be like? You will find that they will help you understand their wants and needs and develop a vision because, at the end of the day, *your clients will do business with you for their reasons, not for yours*!

Remember that even if you created a unique product, you still need to be mindful of the experience that your customers will have with your company. As I said earlier, sooner or later a competitor will come along and attempt to make it better. You need to constantly improve upon what you have, because as soon as you sit still someone is going to reengineer your product or process and improve the experience.

Thinking like an entrepreneur requires continuous reassessment and a feeling that you are never satisfied with the status quo. Think of the goose who laid the golden eggs. We need to take great care of the goose and not kill it by attempting to get the eggs faster by cutting costs or taking shortcuts. The first step to growth means building the top line. There will always be change and challenges, but without the right process in place it will feel like you are running low on time and that life is not what you had hoped. If you have a vision and can put a process in place and create a great experience for your customers, you will get to where you *choose* to go without getting commoditized out of your business.

RESPONSIBLE WEALTH SUMMARY

- *A business needs to create value for others in order to be successful. Differentiate your product or service by the experience you deliver.*
- *A successful leader sets a positive tone, establishes a welcoming experience, and always follows through on promises to customers.*
- *Your customers cannot do everything on their own. If they could, they would not need you. Show respect and patience for their learning.*

CHALLENGING THOUGHTS

- *Do you anticipate that your business could become commoditized? If so, what plans are you making right now to prevent the ramifications of commoditization?*
- *How are you going about building a winning team? In what way are you supporting or enhancing the education and growth of your key employees?*
- *In what ways are you constantly reevaluating your process to improve your customer's experience? How are you collecting feedback from your key employees and top clients?*

Chapter 5

Improving the Bottom Line

Your Future in Business is Determined by Your Bottom Line

Many people spend a lifetime chasing wealth with the belief that net worth is the determining factor in the measurement of wealth. *My observation over the years has proven to me that quality of life directly corresponds to cash flow, and not net worth. Net worth equals assets owned, which are not necessarily available to live on. Cash flow equals income, which is available for enjoyment and quality of life today.* That being the case, it is the most critical aspect of both your personal and business life. To put it bluntly, cash flow will make or break a business. To avoid getting caught in the cash flow trap, you first need to have a solid business plan that includes a budget. I often advise business owners to take courses on budgeting and to get involved with non-profit organizations' financial teams before starting their businesses. This experience will often enable owners to meet some great people with fantastic insight on budgeting and managing cash flow. Within my church's finance committee, each of us has a different background – there is a CPA, retired school administrator, a utility company executive, and me, just to name a few. You will help the organization, learn something, and develop great relationships.

Overall, my advice for keeping control of your bottom line is to project lower revenues than you expect to earn. Creating a budget around lofty sales goals may leave you with an enormous gap in your cash flow – which can cause you to close your doors quickly. And when you itemize expenses, do the opposite: prepare for the worst and hope for the best. This advice is for planning purposes. Of course, if you were providing a financial projection for purposes of a loan, you would want to be as realistic as possible and hedge a little in the other direction to reflect a healthier bottom line. One of my clients had recently promoted a real estate franchise in which he intended to sell homes in this down economy. Due to poor projections, he oversold the ability of his company to investors, and his business was practically bankrupt before it got off the ground. Plan for the worst, hope for the best.

Handling Fixed Cost

Rent, salaries and employee benefits are often the three largest fixed costs inside your budget. Some people assume that they will save money by hiring low salaried employees or operating with fewer employees. I have said a thousand times: Hire the right person for the right job. It will save you time, money and a lot of aggravation. There are many selection tools and tests on the market that will help you determine who will be the right fit. Also, be realistic about what you need from each person. Do not hire someone full-time if there are only twenty hours of work to be completed. Keep your operation efficient, but also provide resources that your employees will need, such as current technology and proper training.

Always treat your team with respect and handle your human capital with care. My investment business manager was recently out of the office for several weeks on medical leave. Because she knows how supportive I am of her and that she has always been treated fairly and respectfully, she was not afraid that her illness would affect her employment. And as soon as she was back to work, she did everything she could to catch up and be extremely productive and helpful. When you have the right people and you treat them the right way, productivity and loyalty follow. The people who work with me know the vision of our organization and are supportive of the goals of the company.

For heaven's sake, don't over-commit and promise the world to your employees! It is nearly impossible to take back perks once they have been given. Once you do something above and beyond, this is now an expectation. Health benefits are a great example of where employers over–commit, then find themselves in the awkward position of eliminating, reducing or passing on the expense of benefits with the rising costs of healthcare. Costs have been rising exponentially over the years. If you have been contributing every dollar toward that cost, then are unable to do so from a budgeting perspective, your employees may not understand this and could resent the cutbacks. I strongly recommend that you continue to look at consumer-driven healthcare approaches such as HMOs, POS and high-deductible medical plans. Consider integrating health reimbursement accounts (HRAs) and health spending accounts (HSAs) into your benefits packages. I believe that, in order to appreciate the value of the benefits, employees should have *skin in the game* – meaning that they should also be expected to contribute financially. It is your responsibility as the employer to make benefits available to your employees, but I do believe that you need to balance this by managing your expenses. In a growing business it is not your responsibility to pay 100 percent. If you do, you will begin to foster the entitlement mentality or support an existing one.

Rewarding Employees

If your employees help you to grow the business or identify cost-saving strategies, reward them! If my associates come to me with a suggestion on how we can save money on telephone usage and help me to research the idea so that we can put it in motion, I will pay them an incentive. So, let's say that I am now saving $500 per month because of the idea – that's $6,000 per year off of my expenses. I might choose to pay out a $500 bonus to them for helping to improve our bottom line.

If you want your workforce to be on the same page, it is very useful to share your vision of where you are trying to go, and to make sure that they know what the company's goals are. If my business produces a certain threshold of revenue in one month, my staff gets a bonus. Depending on how much extra we earned over our projection, that number can increase as targets are hit. If you have a medical office, for example, and notice that your receivables are very high, you might choose to make a deal with your office staff that if they reduce the receivables by, let's says 20 percent, everyone gets a bonus or a free dinner out on you. Some businesses choose to reward efforts by contributing to a retirement account. If you create a culture with your team that says "If I win, we win," you will reduce the entitlement mentality and increase the ownership mentality.

Interestingly, you may find that people with an overall ownership mentality will police their co-workers and help you manage productivity. If you have been promoting open lines of communication, people will be even more likely to bring necessary information to your attention. Work *with* them and give them a feeling of ownership. As your bottom line increases and people are recognized and rewarded, your team will be more loyal to you and the organization.

Keep in mind that programs for rewards can be different based on the diverse groups that you employ. Your office staff may have one type of incentive, but your sales group may be motivated by different benefits. Also, you do not need to focus rewards solely on an individual's successes or contributions. If the entire organization did well, reward the entire team. Remember, on a winning football team, some of the players were standing on the sidelines contributing to the success by way of support. The bottom line is this: you can never say *thank you* enough. You don't need to give away the store every time people do their jobs, but when an exceptional job is done it needs to be acknowledged so that there is incentive to do it again.

Employee Assistance

When people feel content and stress-free in their life outside of work, they will accomplish more when they are at work. That being said, it is very unrealistic to think that you can hire people without any personal challenges or problems. When your best salesman goes home, is he caring for an aging parent? When your assistant leaves for the day, is she frantically trying to care for three children as a single parent? Today, there are many employee assistance programs that can help people. Providing a service will be invaluable to them – getting a handle on challenges will help their overall life and they will be very grateful to you for providing a means to a solution. When you support your employees with the help that they need, you can give them *more than a job, a future*™. Also, the fewer personal issues that are weighing over people's heads, the more productive their workday will be.

Your Accountant

Having a great accountant and CFO can be a very valuable asset to your business's bottom line. People use accountants for bookkeeping services and tax preparation, but their real value lies in their ability to understand your business. They need to provide insight to better enable you to improve the cash flow and bottom line, and their industry expertise should help identify trends in where your money is going and why. You, as a business owner are not the first one ever to be in your particular business – your accountant needs to monitor industry averages. Whether it is outgoing payments for staff, benefits or electricity, your accountant or CFO should keep you up to speed on how you fall in the ranking of other similar businesses and advise you on any necessary corrections.

You need someone who cares, not someone who is trying to sell you products. A word of caution: If your accountant is a product-pusher, be careful. Once he goes from being a consultant to a salesperson, his objectivity is compromised.

A Word To The Wise About Taxes

Make sure that if you are in a business that requires you to pay sales tax you deposit the money as instructed. Payroll tax, sales tax, income tax – whatever it is that you owe – stay out of trouble with the IRS and the state entities because they can make your life miserable. Nonpayment of taxes will result in shutting you down faster than any other business mistake can. Your reputation and integrity is everything when you are in business. One minute you are running your business, the next you are trying to untangle the mess that you have made or come up with the money to bail yourself out because you were not paying attention.

A good accountant should help you keep your business current with all taxes; however, many accountants are rear-view mirror planners. They are great at telling you what has already occurred, but they might not be paying close attention to what is happening presently or going forward. Mind your business and make sure money is released as scheduled.

Complementing Products & Services

Entrepreneurs know that you cannot be all things to all people, so most businesses have a hard time transitioning to other product lines. However, when your fixed costs and overhead are set, adding additional services does not have to increase those costs. (If costs do increase, the increase is usually small compared to the original business start-up cost.) As a financial service organization, my firm does a lot of business with insurance and investments, but we realized that our clients often needed help with mortgages. Since we already had our fixed overhead, we looked to bring in a company to partner with us. They knew their business well, and we knew our clients would be in good hands, so we developed a revenue-sharing arrangement with this mortgage entity.

If you have a medical or health care office and want to add related services and products, you might consider selling items that support good health such as skin lotions or vitamins. If your clients are going to go somewhere else for something that they would be happy to purchase from you, these are where your opportunities lie. Food stores sell shelf space. Think of yourself selling your shelf space because you already have the customers. I do not advocate that a financial company start selling soap. Your solutions need to be complementary to your primary business. I recently had an estimate for the drywall that will be put in my new home that is being built. When the man arrived, he let me know that he and his father had expanded the operation to include insulation and painting, and that he would include a quote to complete all three services. It was a perfect fit.

The best complementary products and services are those that you can incorporate on your own. If the investment of time, money and people would be more expensive than what you would earn, consider teaming up with other people or organizations to create partnerships with them. This way, you can share revenue without investment, and without doing the majority of the work. Lastly, you might consider a strategic alliance with another party if there is an opportunity to mutually refer clients back and forth. Strategic alliances often exist among professionals. Think of fantasy football. You are the quarterback and the client has the chance to patronize the best of each type of professional, based on your recommendation, in order to put the perfect team together. This is a tremendous value-add to your client's experience, one that may enable him to save both time and money.

Document Your Process

The more we document every nuance of our process, the more we recognize that no one person *is* the business. Documenting each person's tasks will allow every role to be defined, so that it may be passed on to another person. So, if my assistant quits, I am not stuck scrambling for the next few months until someone else can figure out what I need accomplished. This concept is not just for employees. If I am out of the office, someone else needs to know what I am supposed to accomplish that day and how to make it happen. Every step that I take a client through is documented in detail so that one of my advanced associates can be trained and prepared to step in if I cannot. Your bottom line increases with these efficiencies, as does your business value.

Did you ever wonder why McDonald's succeeds? People like consistency. Whether you eat at a McDonald's in New Jersey or in Texas, the experience is exactly the same, and so is the hamburger – the order of the cheese, burger, pickles and ketchup is all the same. It is a process that can be duplicated. When you are in the early stages of your career, you are actually doing many of these jobs that you will eventually hire someone to take. This is the time to document every detail. If your process is truly unique, you may want to duplicate it elsewhere. You now have the luxury to grow the business because you can replicate the experience. You might then be in the position to partner or franchise and add locations and revenue streams. Remember: It all ties into whatever your vision is! Having a process also helps you with the hurdles that you will need to work through. A friend told me a long time ago that there are no problems, there are just inconveniences. When one of these inconveniences comes along, you can deal with it as long as you have a process. As someone I know once said, "When you have a process for dealing with a problem, it is not a problem anymore."

Final Thoughts

To impact the bottom line, make sure that everyone on your team is tied into the same goals and objectives. Give them the right perspective, and allow them to feel that they have ownership by rewarding them properly. Avoid the entitlement mentality, in part by making sure that employees are aware of the costs that affect them and that benefits are part of total compensation, not automatic freebies. Again, I do not believe that benefits of retirement are the sole burden of the employer; I believe they are a shared responsibility.

I can tell that people care about our office by both their little and their big contributions. When someone passes by the file room or cafeteria and turns off the lights, or when they remember to turn the heat down when they leave for the day, this shows me that they treat the office like a second home. When you build a culture that cares about the company, everyone wins and you know you are doing something right. When a person refers another person to work at your company or refers a new client, these are also signs of confidence in you and the organization. Reward that person for building the team and building the business.

Employees are one of the largest expenses, so don't rule out being creative with compensation. When your business is young, share your vision with key employees who are hired to help you grow the business. It may be necessary to use less salary and more performance-based compensation plans. If the vision is clear and employees understand where you are going, they just might take the chance with you. Lower your exposure and improve their up-side potential. Motivated people tend to prefer having a greater potential income than to be capped out at a salary anyway.

There was a movie out several years ago called *Field of Dreams* with Kevin Costner. The premise of the movie is: *If you build it, they will come*. That usually does not work as an entrepreneur. That kind of thinking could leave you broke. Before you commit large amounts of time and capital, make sure that the business is going to be there. Work toward your goal, have strategic alliances, but do not jeopardize your future on a guess. Test market products and concepts, and talk to the people in your community. Listen to feedback on what to provide, and for what price. Do your homework before you spend your money. Also, do not operate under the assumption that just because you start something, people will flock to you. The business plan guide in Chapter 8 will help you assess the strength of your new business or expansion idea. Proper planning will leave your business in a position of strength. Finally, be conservative in lifestyle until you are certain that success has arrived.

RESPONSIBLE WEALTH SUMMARY

- *Net worth is all about the assets you own, not about the cash flow you enjoy. Improved quality of life comes by way of improving cash flow.*
- *Hire the right person for the right job, and your investment will be successful.*
- *Share the cost of employee benefits with your employees. This is not a burden you need to carry alone.*
- *Make sure your employees know the company goals and provide incentives when they help reach goals or improve costs.*

CHALLENGING THOUGHTS

- *What relevant training are you providing to your employees? Are you encouraging increased skills and education?*
- *Are you paying all taxes in a timely fashion, and is your accountant keeping you on track? What strategic advice has your accountant provided to you lately?*
- *What plans do you have underway for adding complementary products or services to your business?*
- *What steps have you taken to document your business process?*

Chapter 6

Recognizing Real Assets & Liabilities

Using the Hierarchy of Financial Assets to Your Advantage

Assets enhance your quality of life and are things that retain value. Assets can be time, relationships, health, knowledge, abilities, faith and finances. From a business perspective we can include creativity, key employees, a solid overall staff, intellectual capital and equipment as additional examples. As a productive member of society (not just an entrepreneur), your purpose is to maximize your assets and cultivate them to their highest and best use. Maximization of these assets over your lifetime will allow you to pass them on in a manner that will benefit others in the spirit of generosity and stewardship.

Liabilities take away from or reduce the quality of your life. Liabilities can include a lack of time, health problems, poor relationships, lack of knowledge or education, inabilities, lack of faith and adverse financial circumstances. In the business realm we can add a negative work environment, incompetent or uncommitted staff and no business process to the list. These weaknesses can lead to bad judgment, and if your integrity is not in check, you might cut a corner that leads to big problems – compliance issues, poor quality products and terminating needed staff – which can lead to lost clients and lost revenue. We need to recognize that liabilities can come from many different directions and that they all need to be managed. If the liability causes problems, we need to eliminate it. Liabilities are the direct opposite of assets, and can be a direct downfall of assets.

Hierarchy Of Financial Assets

What do you do if you have extra money? Where does it go? There is no silver bullet that will help you become rich. People have made fortunes by having successful enterprises, only to lose them based on the hope that gambling their fortune in another industry will give them the big windfall. The core principle at the *Institute of Responsible Wealth* is that *you are your greatest asset*. Your ability to think and create is more valuable than anything you can possibly own. Every nuance of who you are makes you your greatest asset.

If we were to identify a hierarchy of financial assets – the order in which your time, effort, and money should be spent – it would be as follows:

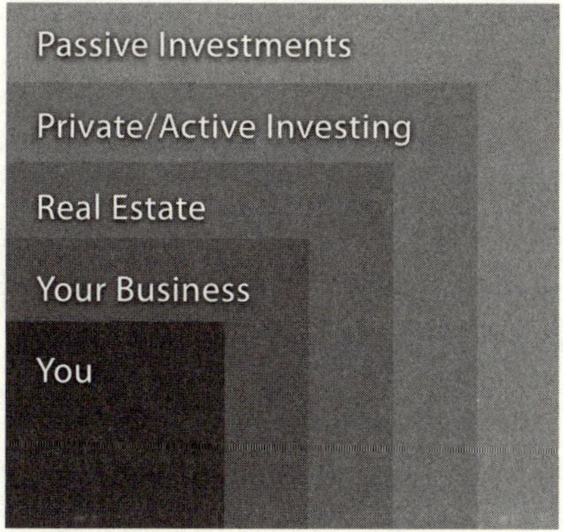

You

The best investment you can make is in yourself. An investment in your knowledge, education, or professional coaching can take your accomplishments to entirely new levels. You are the core of every other money-making decision, and you need to believe in your position as the top of the hierarchy of assets and act accordingly. Recognize and respect your talent, fuel your engine with healthy food and inspiring thought and invest in the asset of you.

Good advisors who have a macro perspective – a *Responsible Wealth Advisor's view* – are a great asset because they can understand the significance of what you are looking to accomplish, and keep you on track. They will reinforce that it all starts with *you*. You and your ability to perform, think creatively and forge relationships are some of your business's greatest assets. The next step is building the right team. If you decide to diversify your investment dollars because you have additional money, your advisor can also help you select a product that is safe and has a favorable rate of return.

I find it ironic that people often treat other investments with more reverence than themselves. They will insure a piece of equipment, but they will not allocate the premiums to insure themselves for liability, death or disability. They will invest hard-earned dollars in passive investments (the lowest opportunity) instead of into their own business and education. Keep in mind that without you, none of the other things exist. It is your passion, personality and intelligence that create the revenue to invest anywhere else, to purchase anything else and to care for anyone else.

Your Business

Your business represents how you create value and provide service to others. Your business is also the vehicle through which you build your own wealth. I invest in education, marketing and advertising my business, adding more experienced employees to my company, and training my staff. You might hire a salesperson, controller or business manager who will help improve the company's bottom line. You could also add more equipment to produce more widgets or a higher quality of goods. The key is to identify dollars and resources that you can invest toward the growth of your own company. People have long believed that owning stocks are the best investment, but wouldn't the stock in your own company make more sense? In a country where most of our millionaires are closely held business owners, it makes the most sense to put your time and money where you will get the greatest return on them. As an entrepreneur, you should look at every opportunity to grow personally or grow your business. Remember: You can be your best investment.

Building the business is simply creating the process by which you deliver your originality. When you put the details of the process together, you get to decide whether you want to sell licensing, start a franchise, or do it all on your own. The decisions are limitless, and they are yours to make. I had lunch recently with a client in the restaurant/bar industry. Before he went into business for himself, he worked for a major bar/restaurant group. His job was to determine suitable areas for new locations and get each facility up and running. He did this for several years, and finally chose to go out on his own. He is a relatively young man who has taken his knowledge and built his own wealth, not someone else's. Ten years later, he owns fifteen successful bar/restaurants and he is still growing his business. He learned the formula for a process that worked, he put the ball in motion, and replicated the process over and over again.

A bank in the Northeast called Commerce Bank (now T.D. Bank) did just that in their world; they developed a process that was different and they replicated it. They started with just one branch that had some unique characteristics, such as being open on Sundays, then grew into a bank with hundreds of branches, and were recently acquired by a larger bank. You can take your unique process and sell it, sell licenses for it, or stay in business to make money. *That* is how you build *Responsible Wealth*.

Real Estate (Passive Income)

Real estate is the next area on the hierarchy of building wealth. Many entrepreneurs add another layer to their portfolio of assets by owning the real estate that houses their business. Instead of paying rent to someone else, they pay themselves and grow a separate asset in addition to their businesses. This may provide tax and other benefits that are not available in passive investments. They might also invest in other real estate projects, such as investment homes or commercial buildings to diversify their passive income. This does not include speculative projects; I am referring to quality, income-producing real estate only.

Private Equity

Private equity is typically an investment not sold through traditional means. For a private equity investment to be a sound financial decision, my advice is that you either know someone or something about the type of investment you are considering. Does the person with whom you are entrusting your hard-earned dollars have expertise in the given area? If you are a restaurateur and you are approached to be an investor in another restaurant, you may want to participate in the project if they have a good business plan. You can add value and capital, and you will have confidence that the risk is mitigated because of their business acumen, combined with your overall contribution. The opportunity in private equity is in being a part of a project that you do not have to manage entirely on your own, but one that you can potentially earn a significant rate of return for your contribution. Many private equity investments are not available to everyone, and may have financial qualifications required before you can invest. There also are private equity programs marketed to the public. In my opinion, these have greater risks and your insight will be limited to a prospectus and/or business memorandum.

Passive Investments

Passive investments are bank accounts, certificates of deposit (CDs), annuities, stocks, bonds, and mutual funds. As it relates to those investments, the majority of us are investing as outsiders. We have limited knowledge of the company and only have access to information that everyone else knows. These investments are really no more than inflation-adjusted holding tanks. Herein lies the challenge for an entrepreneur: If you are to look at the hierarchy of what is available to invest in, the best investment is you, and the worst investment is the group of passive investment choices. Many business owners who are successful in *their own* businesses attempt, unsuccessfully, to get rich in *someone else's* business. This means that they take money, which is fuel for the future growth of their own company, and they speculate in other markets (such as the stock market, i.e. someone *else's* business) and possibly lose their hard-earned money. When you invest in a public company, you have no control of the success or failure; thus you are subject to speculation and a hope that the price will go up.

Interestingly, the financial service community primarily exists by offering investments in this last category. Because there is a perception that business owners have a lot of disposable cash, investment advisors and stockbrokers are often soliciting their business to invest in the financial markets. If I were to invest in the stock market, I would be investing in someone else's business, not my own. Overall, when we choose to invest in any business that we do not understand or cannot control, we are often speculating, not investing. Furthermore, these products are disguised as diverse, when in fact they are not. They are often all correlated assets and all tend to move in the same direction with the market. Diversification exists when you have non-correlated assets. For example, an investment account of precious metals (gold, silver), cash, some stocks and real estate would be an example of diversification of non-correlated assets. If one goes down, they tend not to all go down. Unfortunately, many financial representatives do not hold licenses to sell products of different types, so they do not offer this as a solution to their clients. They suggest to clients that they are using asset allocation, when they really need to be directing clients to diversify in non-correlated assets.

Financial professionals rarely address other, better investments such as investing in yourself, in your business, in real estate and in private equity for similar reasons – they do not get paid for this. They would have you believe that parking all of your money in one place (such as the stock market) is the most prudent decision, and that if you give them all of your money you will be rich years later by some miracle that they have performed. Overall, the idea that you will become wealthy by investing in passive investments is a fallacy. I am not saying that passive investments are all bad; they are a good way to diversify into different asset classes, or to diversify into non-correlated areas. It may be a suitable place to store your money until a better opportunity comes along. Unfortunately, the financial institutions are often marketing this area as the best place for your money, and as an entrepreneur this is not necessarily true or prudent. Taking money out of circulation for long periods of time subjects your money to infinite opportunity costs. Financial publications are often touting the benefits of these products, but most of these articles and magazines are nothing more than paid advertisements. They are an infomercial, nothing more.

Often when I meet with my business owner clients, they ask me about investments. Before going into the pros and cons of passive investments and the financial institutions that sell them, I always ask about the rate of return they earn in their business. What is their return on capital? Some people look at me as if that is a strange question. When I find that rates of return are significantly higher than averages in the market, I then ask, "Why in the world would you want to use another vehicle to earn money when your business reinvestment can get you up to *double* that rate of return?" One client, a real estate developer, did tell me that under the current market conditions he could not find an opportunity to invest in, so this was an acceptable way to manage the money until the next project came along. That is one of the right reasons to diversify.

Putting The Hierarchy To Work

A friend and client is the chairman of the board for a bank. One day, I asked him if he was open to talking about investments. He said to me, "Frank, I only own one stock. I own stock in the bank I am a founder in." When you understand that your greatest possibilities are in the areas that you can control and that you personally understand, your financial decisions will come much more easily to you. You may have listened to Warren Buffett speak about investing, but be aware that he does not just own a few stocks. He buys such a large position in a company that he is often represented on the board of directors and has an understanding about the direction of the company. He has access to the inner workings of the organization. The average investor has no clue what he/she is investing in, and neither does the stockbroker or advisor who is selling products or shares. And when was the last time your financial representative made sure that you knew that the mutual funds you were buying were just paper, and that you own no actual stock at all?

The sooner you understand the hierarchy of financial assets and can put the concept in motion, the more accelerated your growth becomes. Your ability to focus changes. You stop thinking that it is possible to move money to get rich. Think of *The Wizard of Oz*. At the end of the movie, Dorothy clicks her heels and says, "There's no place like home." In retrospect, many people realize that they should have just kept their money "at home" in their own business all along. There is so much marketing to convince us to lock up our money with financial institutions, but as entrepreneurs we need to have the courage and confidence in our own ingenuity to keep investing in ourselves.

Living Within Your Means Preserves Your Assets

My friend Peter was very successful at one point and had the lifestyle to prove it. Unfortunately, the bottom fell out of his business and he began living a life that he was not particularly proud of. He learned many valuable lessons during this period, and one day he heard someone say that EGO stands for Edging God Out. He had been so obsessed with himself – what he deserved to have, what he did wrong, what he wanted out of life – and he knew it. The lack of balance was abundantly clear. His orchestra was now more of a one-man band. Once you lose the focus on what you want to accomplish and why, your road to ruin is a quick one, no matter how long it took to build success.

A life out of harmony tends to have increased liabilities. Liabilities are a major cause of distraction, or *diffusion*. And *diff*usion leads to *con*fusion. Having the inability to focus makes it hard to pick up the pieces and turn around the irresponsible behavior. You have added so much pressure to yourself by setting bad precedents at home and in business, and you might be constantly worried that your business might not be able to survive the hard times. You might be wondering: Where and when can I borrow money?

Borrowing money is technically taking on a liability, which is acceptable as long as the purpose is ultimately to acquire or grow an asset. A mortgage on a house can build an asset of real estate. A loan for a new piece of equipment might help you manufacture more products to sell. If one offsets the other, you are probably making an investment and not borrowing for consumption. As long as the return on investment can be seen, this is an investment. Borrowing for consumption is a liability that has no benefits. Recently, I borrowed money from the bank to increase the size of my office building, which has allowed me to increase staff and add a new business unit, but I would never recommend or even consider borrowing money to take a fancy vacation or to purchase depreciating assets such as cars, televisions and so on.

You *and your family* need to live within your means. It is easy to get carried away by periods of financial success and the need to tell everyone how well business is going by way of the things that we buy. Having a big house and a fancy car is nice as long as it is living below your means. There are lots of big houses out there with barely any furniture inside. Chances are those people are over-leveraged. You earn money so that you can enjoy life, but the moment that lifestyle represents ego, you are headed for trouble. Lifestyle can become our biggest distraction because it starts a vicious cycle of taking us away from the very business that supports it. Everyone in your household needs to know enough about the financial goals of the family to work together to achieve them. If your spouse is forever nagging you about going on more expensive vacations or buying other consumer products, he/she is hurting the end-result by taking more time and money away from the business. As an entrepreneur, I am a producer first, then a consumer. By living within my means, I am able to enjoy my wealth in a way that is on par with my income. Communicate your goals to your family so they help to build your family assets and legacy.

Proverbs 12, Verse 11 effectively tells us "he who tills his fields will be satisfied with bread, but he who follows frivolity is devoid of understanding."

My purpose in explaining assets and liabilities, as well as the Hierarchy of Financial Assets, is this: Do not be swayed by financial institutions and the mass media into thinking that their way is the best way. Just because your neighbors invest with the herd does not mean that you have to give up your financial rights and follow them off the cliff. Certainly, if you are an entrepreneur, your best asset will always be YOU. And, if you are teetering on the line of becoming an entrepreneur, your best investment is still probably YOU! In this country, people do not become wealthy by tucking money under a mattress or accepting second best – a low return on their money. Financially, the big wins will come from creativity, ingenuity and a lot of dedication. Be active, not passive, and have fun with your success. Do not live in fear – live in inspiration!

RESPONSIBLE WEALTH SUMMARY

- *Assets increase the value of your life and help you achieve your goals, whereas liabilities detract from your ability to succeed.*
- *Under the Hierarchy of Assets, YOU are the most important financial asset in which to invest.*
- *Once you learn the formula that works, you can repeat the process and continue to increase your successful enterprises.*
- *Living below or within your means will preserve your assets. By keeping your ego in check, you will not be tempted to let your lifestyle outpace your cash flow.*

CHALLENGING THOUGHTS

- *What are the most significant assets that are helping you grow your business or start up a new endeavor?*
- *What are the most significant liabilities that need to be addressed or eliminated because they could sabotage your business?*
- *How do you plan to invest in YOU over the course of the next year? Have you written your five-year business plan?*

Chapter 7

Business Plans & Financing

How to be Bankable

One of my mentors, Tim, taught me early in my career that you make money in your business and you lose money in everyone else's. When you choose to invest, first look in your own backyard. As I explained in the Hierarchy of Financial Assets in Chapter 6, you and your business are the top two places to make investments and will likely yield the highest return on investment. Don't be convinced to invest in some mutual fund portfolio just because a salesman comes along with a glossy brochure and you are having a bad day at work.

As business owners, we have to continue to be aware of our opportunities. When we don't, this is truly what is meant by opportunity cost. An opportunity cost occurs when there are two investment vehicles and you choose the one with the lesser return. I will warn you to be very conscious of time. It might appear that one investment is better, but based on the amount of time your money is tied-up, it may not be what it originally appears to be. When you have a new business idea or a plan for expansion of your existing business, you always need to start with a business plan. This will take you through the proper steps of assessing the success of an idea. Once you have decided to proceed, then you are ready to select the method of funding. Your financing can and probably will change over time and the original way in which you get the money might be refinanced or restructured. The goal is to obtain the money to get the project off the ground.

A Business Plan

If you are going to start or expand a business, you must have a business plan. Without the details in writing, you appear to be a dreamer, making it difficult, if not impossible, for you to finance your endeavor. Once you take the idea to paper, it becomes an investment, and you are ready to determine the funding strategy. Here is a basic overview of the business plan components:

- *What is the core product?* It does not need to be the best product. The most successful coffeehouses do not have the best cup of coffee.

- *What is the core service, or the core value that you are bringing to the public?*

- *Research the market.*
  - Who is the consumer for your product or service?
  - Is there a market for it?
  - Is there a need or desire for this concept? Is there an audience?
  - Who is the competition?
  - Where is the potential marketplace?
  - Will people pay for the product or service?
- *How would you market the product or service to the consumer?* Lay out the details as specifically as possible.
- *Budget Analysis.* Do your homework and use real numbers. Find an accounting firm that specializes in your idea or your field to use their research and experience. They will disclose items that you might not have brainstormed on your own.
- *Prepare a budget.*
  - Projection of sales
    - Minimum – worst-case scenario
    - Expected return
    - Maximum – best-case scenario
  - Projection of expenses
    - Maximum – worst-case scenario
    - Expected return
    - Minimum – best-case scenario
  - Number of employees needed
    - Cost of salary and total compensation including taxes
    - Benefits to be provided to them

- Cost of space
    - Square feet needed to operate
    - Rent, lease, or buy?

- Utilities
    - Gas
    - Electric
    - Telephone
    - Cellular phones
    - Cable if necessary
    - Water

- Cost of goods

- Cost of services

- *Raise the capital.* You can raise capital in the form of borrowing (debt) or partnering with an investor (equity). Having a good accountant lends tremendous credibility when you raise capital, regardless of which method you choose.

Raising Capital Using Debt

If you, as an entrepreneur, have a great idea, my recommendation is to first consider borrowing money to fund it versus giving up an equity stake in your company. Why would you want to give up ownership if you don't have to? If the money can be borrowed at a reasonable rate of interest, there is no need to sacrifice ownership.

Having a good banking relationship can be key in obtaining money. Community banks are an outstanding resource. They will give you the ability to talk to an officer who will have the time to listen to you and get to know you and your idea. They have an interest in making an investment in you and your business. They will get to know you on a personal basis because they are really buying *you*. If they do not trust you, or your numbers do not back up your project; they will probably not lend to you.

A bank may choose to lend you money because of the greater relationship that you can provide to them. Perhaps you need a loan to expand your operation and you agree to move all of your accounts to their branch. If your business was responsible for tens or hundreds of thousands of dollars each month, this could impact them and their decision tremendously. It might make the difference of them funding your loan or rejecting your application. Some banks might even be more competitive on the rate of your loan if you agree to funnel your credit card business to them, or establish a line of credit. Banks make money when they hold your money and utilize it in their system. Don't ever forget that.

Early on in my business ownership, I decided to buy a real estate lot to build a building. At that time, the real estate market was very soft and I came across a lot that had been foreclosed upon. I learned very quickly that the bank I used owned this property, and I began negotiations to buy the lot from them. When they presented their original price to me, it was about double what I was willing to pay. As conversations went on, I explained that I had planned to build an office complex; when the time came for construction, I would finance that commercial loan with them. In addition, I assured them that I planned to continue banking with them. Due to the total relationship that I was able to create in addition to that one piece of property, I purchased the building for half of what they originally had requested as a sales price. Although this negotiation is more likely to occur with a small bank than a large, publically owned bank, this was a very personal reminder of how banks make money. They make money from holding our money and using it to lend to others over and over again. My bank knew that they would earn more by keeping me as a client than they would on one single transaction.

A little-known fact is that insurance and investment companies are another source for mortgages. I even inquired about a mortgage for my own commercial building from two insurance companies, but the loan size was not large enough for them. Mortgages are often core holdings for insurance and investment companies' portfolios of long-term assets.

When securing a loan, a lender will want to have two questions answered: (1) How are you going to secure the loan? (If you don't pay, how will they get their money back?) and (2) How are you going to make the payments? Your own credibility is a component of raising capital, both your financial credibility and a resume of your business experience. In most start-up ventures, you will often have to personally guarantee the loan, and any lender will want to feel confident that you are likely and able to repay the loan. They will look at your income and personal assets. If you are financially strong, you will personally guarantee assets that you already own as collateral for the loan. If you are not strong financially, a bank might choose to take your loan and hold it within its portfolio. If a bank is not sure that you fit into its lending criteria, it may recommend a loan backed by the Small Business Association (SBA), not entirely by the bank itself. The SBA program is designed to assess the applicant's character, credit, experience and reliability, rather than assets, and acts as the guarantor of a loan given by that bank. Smaller banks, however, may not be SBA-preferred lenders. This might limit your use of this product to larger, more experienced institutions.

Banks are not always the best places to go for money. You may want to interview a few commercial loan brokers who can help provide alternatives, or you might find individual investors (or groups of investors) who want the opportunity to loan money privately, in exchange for a rate of return on that money. The terms of the loan and the type of involvement would be determined by both parties. Years ago, a client was looking to expand his printing company and was approached by a retired executive from Wall Street who was looking for an investment. The Wall Street investor took a liking to both the investment and the business itself, and decided to buy into the printing company as a part-owner. He was younger than the original owner, and years later he purchased the entire company from him. There are investors of all kinds who actively seek opportunities to fund entrepreneurs. Another client sold his business for millions, then he went on to invest and coach new business owners in their projects. Then there is my friend Larry, who enjoys the challenge of taking on mortgages for businesspeople who are not able to obtain them through traditional mortgage lenders; he takes on this addition risk for a higher rate of interest when the loan-to-value ratio is higher than normal. This way, if the borrower defaults, he will be somewhat secure in his position. Sometimes Larry also will ask the borrower to pledge other collateral, or even have a secondary guarantee from a co-signer.

On a personal note, some years ago a group of investors invited me to become a shareholder in a project to build a nursing home in my local area. By the time they came to my conference room to present the details, they had about ten people signed up to invest, including an attorney, an accountant, a doctor and several builders. After meeting with the group, I declined ownership participation in the project because there was not one person at the table who had ever been in the nursing home business. Their business plan had holes in it, and their budgets seemed unrealistic. This was a red flag to me, and the success of the ongoing business seemed unlikely. However, they were at the point in the project where they were about to close on the land and I offered to hold the mortgage on the land for a favorable rate of interest. I held that mortgage for a number of years, and they never did get the nursing home built. In the end, I made money holding the note and the other investors still have not gotten their money back.

Raising Capital Using Equity

Entrepreneurs choose to offer an equity position for financing expansion or start-up ventures in two circumstances: They cannot borrow the money at a reasonable rate of interest, or their idea is speculative and they want to mitigate the risk among other parties. Unlike in raising capital with debt, there is no personal guarantee when you offer an equity position. The money is secured solely by ownership in the business. If the money is for purposes of expansion, be certain to review all of your existing lending arrangements to ensure that there is no conflict in extending an equity position to anyone else. Some bank loans are collateralized based on your ownership of the business at the time of the loan, so adding another shareholder could trigger the loan to be called.

There are many sources of equity. Depending on the scope of the project, you may choose to add a working partner to your company, take your company public, or offer the opportunity to invest to your key employees. I have some close friends who are minority shareholders in the company for which they work. You might also choose to be funded by venture capitalists, angel investors, a hedge fund or private investors. (As an aside, I would discourage the use of family money as a first-line source of funding because it is very difficult to sit across from someone at Thanksgiving dinner if you have lost their money.) You can even open a copy of the *Wall Street Journal* and find investors looking for opportunities. Some investors choose to have very little involvement, and others are very involved in the operation. The terms of the finances and involvement will be determined before any money is exchanged.

Private equity investors are going to assess a risk factor, which determines your cost to borrow based upon the risk they perceive. If they feel that you are credit-worthy and that the business idea has a high probability of succeeding, the risk premium is going to be low. If they feel that you and/or your idea are questionable, they will assess a high-risk premium. On the public side, there is a rating system that allows an investor to know about a company's strength and creditworthiness. If one was rated AAA and another was rated C, you as an investor would know that you would need to earn a higher return on a C-rated company to make the risk worthwhile. Although not as formal, investors assess you in a similar fashion. If you have had trouble paying your bills in the past or have money of your own to invest, they would need to earn a higher return to mitigate their risk investing in you.

When you are ready to move forward with your start-up or expansion, it is best to come to the financing table with good credit, a thorough business plan, and realistic expectations and budgets. To determine whether debt or equity is preferable, choose the cheapest money in the short-run *and* the long-run. You might just realize that borrowing money from your own assets is the most beneficial. You may have a stock portfolio to margin, or even cash value in your life insurance. If possible, choose to borrow money before offering an equity position. If you believe deeply in your idea, do not give up a piece of its ownership to another party too quickly. You will be sorry the day you sell the company and lose a large portion of your proceeds to someone else because they own shares. Keep in mind that a good accountant lends credibility when you raise capital. Not only will they help you prepare the budget and financial statements, but they might also have banking relationships, and be able to introduce you to the right people.

Many endeavors fail because they are underfunded, so be certain that you are realistic with your cost projections, and build in extra money where possible. If you are involved in a construction project, anticipate that each phase will be more expensive than projected, and ask for more money than you need. Do not spend it unnecessarily, but have it available in case you run over on cost. This way the construction will continue and time will not elapse as you wait for your bank to reassess lending you more capital.

If your business plan is to purchase an existing business that you can make more profitable, consider that the current owner may be open to retaining a debt or equity position in the company. This can be especially beneficial for you because the private agreement might be easy to obtain, because the investor might already know the business. You would be able to use bank financing to expand, as long as you qualify otherwise. Overall, analyze whether the money can be obtained at a more competitive rate of return before making a decision to proceed in this manner. If your local bank's money will be cheaper in the long-run, you might still choose a bank loan.

When a business is sold, money simply changes its holding tank. Most of the time, a prior owner will simply move the money out of the business and into a passive investment portfolio which is subject to market risk. As we learned from the Hierarchy of Financial Assets, there is no greater investment than you or your business, so it would be very logical for the original owner to continue to keep his money in a place he trusts. An owner might choose to hold paper and have you make payments in the form of an annuity (debt) or remain a shareholder (equity). The sale might even be structured as an installment sale, allowing the original owner to avoid paying taxes on the entire gain in one given year. The tax liability would be spread out as payments were made.

Final Thoughts

In funding *The Institute of Responsible Wealth*, I had a variety of choices. After careful consideration, I chose to use my personal capital because, for me, this was the cheapest money. Had my money been in a market earning 15, 20 or 30 percent, I would have chosen financing from a bank or partners instead. Due to the current market conditions, however, I felt I would get the best rate of return on my money by investing in me. I have a vision, I know where the project is going and I believe in my success. The strength of you and your business plan will make or break your success in your start-up or expansion. Be as thorough as possible when creating a budget. Obtain the cheapest money to finance the project, and do not hesitate to be creative. There are many ways to accomplish your dream, and you might need to be persistent!

RESPONSIBLE WEALTH SUMMARY

- *You make money in your business, so when you are looking for an investment, first choose your own business before someone else's.*
- *A business plan is your roadmap for success and will ensure that you have done due diligence on your business idea. It will allow a bank to see your idea and be part of the package which determines whether you will receive a loan.*
- *There are other types of financing available besides traditional banks. Consider whether using a private investor will help you fund your business or expansion, and weigh the option of using debt or equity to repay their investment.*

CHALLENGING THOUGHTS

- *Have you thoroughly researched your idea for your business plan? Have you incorporated the thoughts of experts in the field, as well as financial advisors such as your accountant?*
- *Why will people use your product or service? Have you done market research?*
- *What type of relationship do you have with your bank or lending institution?*

Chapter 8

Protecting Real Assets

Keeping Business Assets & Personal Assets Safe

When you are a business owner, you have a lot on the line to protect. It is essential to protect yourself because you are the engine that keeps everything moving forward, and it is also vital to protect your assets from creating a liability for which you are responsible. This chapter will discuss strategies necessary to create layers of protection for your assets in your world as an entrepreneur.

Part I: Protecting Your Business Assets

Forms of Entity

Your business may be the largest asset that you own. There are two main concerns you as an entrepreneur need to address for this significant asset: (1) you will want to create the most favorable tax treatment possible and (2) you *must* insulate yourself properly from liability. Choosing the right type of business entity allows you to accomplish these two necessary steps. Deciding which entity to choose is a little like picking out a new house. A good advisor will help you select what type of roof to have over your head, and should be able to tell you when you have outgrown your existing residence. A good advisor will also help determine when you need separate business entities for other things you will own such as real estate or equipment. This way, when you choose to sell one item, you don't have to sell the entire house in which you live.

When you form an entity, be mindful of the rules of engagement. Each has its own rules for recordkeeping, expense write-offs, documentation, ownership and operating agreements, etc. If you are not obeying the rules and you set up a business entity for the advantages of one type (for example, tax treatment), but you combine it with the advantages of another (for example, writing off personal expenses), you can find yourself up a creek without a paddle if you were ever named in a lawsuit or investigated by the IRS. You may find that someone can *pierce the corporate veil* and take away the level of protection that you thought you had. If your entity is breaking the rules, and is not operating as it is registered, then you will likely not receive the built-in protection. You may have heard the expression: *If it walks like a duck and talks like a duck, chances are it's a duck*. Well, make sure you stay a duck. When you select your entity with your accountant and attorney, make sure you are planning to be consistent with the rules of the entity. Other rules that also need to be abided by are keeping the minutes at each meeting and operating out of a corporate checkbook without comingling business money with personal funds.

To stick with our analogy, your advisor, accountant and attorney might also suggest you establish another house – another entity – for separation of assets. For example, your office building and your expensive equipment might be separated from your business itself. This way, each entity can have its own ownership protection and profit and loss. And if a lawsuit were to occur with one company or against a piece of property, it would not typically implicate the others. There are some tax-planning strategies at work here as well. If one business pays rent or leases equipment from another, passive income is generated, which is more favorable than earned income.

The type of entity that you choose should be selected carefully, and I advise you to consult with your accountant and attorney for a thorough analysis of pros and cons of each entity. The following will provide a brief overview of the types:

Sole Proprietor

A personally held business starts and ends with you, and you are responsible for everything in between. The advantage to this entity is its simplicity to set up. The disadvantage is that if you are ever sued, you have no insulation or protection between your entity and your personal financial life. A sole proprietorship ends upon your demise, and cannot be continued by the next generation.

Partnership

A partnership is an agreement between two or more individuals, groups of individuals, companies or corporations where profits and expenses are shared. The advantage is that it is simple to set up. Similar to the sole proprietorship, this type of business arrangement provides no level of liability protection and no additional tax planning strategies.

Regular Corporation

If your business will be profitable right away, your accountant might suggest a regular corporation for purposes of shifting income. This will provide the ability to leave income inside of the business to be taxed at one bracket, and distribute other income to you as a shareholder to be taxed at your personal bracket. Larger companies are typically taxed in this fashion, or set up with this form of entity.

Retained earnings, the earnings left inside the corporation, will be taxed at the corporate level. If that is not to your benefit, choose a flow-through entity that allows you to take all of the income or losses into your personal income for tax purposes. This form of entity can provide liability protection and may be continued upon your demise.

S-Corporation

Younger, newly established companies tend to be set up as flow-through entities such as s-corporations. Many older companies over the last several years have chosen to convert to s-corporations status due to individual income tax rates being similar or lower than corporate tax rates. Accountants often recommend s-corporations for businesses that may experience losses because of the ability to have any losses flow-through to the personal side and act as a write-off for the individual which is more favorable. Each owner in an s-corporation has a specific number of shares of the corporation, and distributions of profits or losses are distributed to all shareholders. The profits show up on corporate tax returns in the form of a K-1, and the s-corporation issues a 1099 to the owners in the amount of the income generated by the company based on the number of shares the individual owns. S-corporations do provide protection from liability, as shareholders may not be responsible for the debts of the corporation. Like a regular corporation, the business can be continued after your demise.

LLC, LLP, & FLP

Limited Liability Companies, Limited Liability Partnerships, and Family Limited Partnerships are similar to s-corporations in their ability to act as flow-through entities. And, like s-corporations, they do provide a level of protection from liability and can be continued upon a partner's demise. This form of entity is often easier to keep in compliance than traditional corporations.

Agreements

Once the business entity is established and you buy some fancy letterhead from the local printer, you might think you are in business. Not quite yet! When there is more than one person involved with ownership of a company, it is essential to address certain issues prior to any situation arising. Leave no room for assumptions as it pertains to each person's responsibilities, levels of compensation, and the process of exiting the company (whether voluntary or involuntary). If items such as these are not put in writing from the beginning, you may never put agreements in place, which can lead to serious problems when situations occur. The rules need to be out in the open so that each player is well informed.

If you have partners or shareholders in your business, you need an agreement that spells out precisely how your business will function and the responsibilities of each person. In corporations, this is called a *shareholders' agreement*. (In other entities, these are known as a *partnership* agreement or *operating* agreement.) These agreements stipulate responsibilities of each shareholder or partner, share distribution, compensation agreements, and the process you will follow if a shareholder exits the business for any reason, among other things. The exit strategy and all things related to the transfer of shares/ ownership (also known as a *buy-sell agreement*) are items to which you want to pay particular attention. A member may choose to retire or sell his interest, or, in the event of a disability or death during working years a plan needs to be in place. Many different scenarios can arise, and each needs to be addressed in advance of its occurrence.

The *business valuation* is at the heart of the shareholders' agreement and the buy-sell agreement as it pertains to transfer of shares for any reason. Depending upon your business type and your industry, there are many different ways to value a business. Your *Responsible Wealth Advisor* and your accountant can guide you through the process. Once you have a formula for valuation, you will need to determine if your company will self-insure or transfer the risk elsewhere in the event you need to take over another person's shares.

Self-insuring essentially means that you have no insurance, and that you can afford to absorb this expenditure on any given day. Your company will assume the entire responsibility in the event that a loss of a shareholder occurs for any reason. One type of self-insuring method is known as a *sinking fund*, which is a system of depositing money into a fund reserved for such an event. Although this method can work, it has two pitfalls – it ties up a significant amount of capital over the years, and if the claim comes before the account has enough money, you may wind up with a shortage of cash on hand. Another method of self-insuring is via financing the obligation through a bank. You would pay the former shareholder (or former shareholder's family, if the shareholder dies) the lump sum and finance the payments with interest. Overall, using insurance is the best method for funding an agreement. The insurance company will assess the risk and charge you a premium for taking on the liability. Even if you were willing to take on the risk of absorbing the cost (via a sinking fund or a financing), this would be a less efficient use of your money.

Property & Casualty Insurance

When it comes to liability protection for your business, it pays to insure yourself by every means available. To protect against mistakes that you could potentially make in your line of business, some industries have *malpractice* insurance and others have *errors and omissions* coverage. In the event that a lawsuit is filed against you, this liability protection is there to cover a loss or a judgment.

Insurance for real estate and equipment is known as *property insurance* and should be acquired for full replacement value of these assets, with deductibles that are financially feasible for you. It typically will not be the deductible that will wipe you out, it will be the big loss that you just cannot afford that will make you suffer. It always strikes me as ridiculous when I hear people say that if they incurred a significant loss, they would simply file for bankruptcy and just start over again. That is not what you went into business to do. Your integrity and reputation as a business owner will never be the same.

An additional layer of liability protection for your business is known as *business excess insurance* or an *umbrella policy*. To protect against the threat of exposure to lawsuits that exceed your existing business auto insurance, general liability insurance, or other liability insurances, an umbrella policy picks up where the other coverages leave off. You will find that having this additional coverage is quite inexpensive in comparison to the consequences of a need arising and not having it in place. Due to the nature of our highly litigious society, it is better to be safe than sorry.

Income Replacement & Disability Planning

Replacement value on your buildings and real estate is vital, but protecting your other most important assets – yourself and your key employees – is also crucial. You are your business's greatest asset due to your work ethic, relationships, creativity and ingenuity, to name just a few characteristics. This can be accomplished through disability insurance and life insurance.

If you are in business for yourself and you do not have partners or other shareholders, it is still essential to have adequate insurance to protect yourself and/or your own family if you suffer a disability or premature death. Otherwise, your family may have little hope of replacing the value of *you* from the assets of the business. Without you, the engine of the business, your operation may cease to exist altogether. And if the marketability of your particular product or service is not that strong, your family may need to sell the business at a time when it could be worth pennies on the dollar. Imagine your life's work being virtually meaningless without you there? Insuring *yourself* will guarantee the full value to your family and prevent the financial loss of years of hard work.

I will go into great detail about personal disability insurance later in this chapter, however, I would like to address the harsh reality of disability as it affects your business. People do not stop being consumers while waiting for you to get well. If your business relies primarily on your talents, your customers are likely to move their business elsewhere without you in the picture. Whether or not profits start to waiver, your employees will probably begin their job search in short order because they know that their employment could be in jeopardy. People never want to risk being left without their income. Having *key person disability insurance* is vital if the operation relies on one or a few key people's talents. A claim through insurance will fund your business's ability to hire someone to take on your role or another's role and replace lost revenue.

Other forms of disability insurances can also help keep your business operational in the event of a disability. *Business overhead expense* insurance will provide the capital to pay all or a portion of your business expenses, such as employee salaries, rent, utilities, benefit costs, and possibly even key person replacement, during the period of lost revenue. These benefits are typically paid for a limited period of time, usually one to two years, but they give you time to recover and keeps your life's work intact until you can come back from your claim. Additionally, there are disability insurances that will repay loans that are outstanding (such as a buyout loan, employment contract, or mortgage) directly to the payee. These types of coverage will protect not just your business interest in keeping your company afloat, but will also protect your staff from being forced to leave and your credit from being destroyed due to the non-payment of obligations.

Life Insurance

Life insurance is money delivered in the future upon your demise and at a time when it might be most needed. The cash value inside of life insurance can act as one of your non-correlated assets, which we touched on in Chapter 6 under Passive Investments. Cash value does not go through the normal economic cycles that your business, stock market or real estate market might experience. Another benefit of cash value is that it can be a cash reserve that you have available to you for other opportunities. In my field of expertise, I sometimes hear people say, "I don't need life insurance." On this topic, I have taken wise advice from my friend Tim who is also an advisor. Tim says that whenever you say the words *life insurance*, you should replace it with the word *money*. This changes the statement from "I don't need *life insurance*," to "I don't need *money*." If you do need money, and you do want money to be delivered at some point in the future, you have already made the decision to incorporate life insurance into your overall plan, which will give you far greater security and flexibility in the future.

In the same way that you insure your property and liability, you should also insure the life of yourself and your key employees. Without these people in the picture, your business could potentially suffer substantial financial loss. ALL insurances should be properly in place, not just some. Key person life insurance is just as essential for you and your key officers as disability insurance, and for similar reasons. If you have personally guaranteed notes or loans, there needs to be enough money to pay off all business debts so that your estate does not become liable for the debt if you die prematurely. There is no need for your family to incur liens on your personal estate because of a lack of planning. Also, your key employees' and officers' lives should be insured, because if you lose an essential member of your company, it will likely be difficult to replace that person's talents before a loss of revenue occurs.

Among other things, *Responsible Wealth* means protecting your wealth as you build it. If a loss occurs, you do not want to give up the wealth you have accumulated. So, the process is this: You grow, you protect, you grow larger, you protect more. Protection is an ongoing reassessment as your assets grow. It would be no different if you were buying stock. If the stock is going up, personally I would periodically put a stop-loss on the investment to make sure I do not give up my earnings. Otherwise, you might as well just sit at a casino table and say, "I'm all in." As a business owner, you are not in the game of speculating. Responsible entrepreneurs build and protect their assets, and they also recognize that their assets are not just their equipment. Their assets are their integrity, the business itself and the people – themselves and their key employees.

Let's say that you as the business owner are fortunate enough to live a long, healthy life. If you can imagine, dream of yourself as someone who not only lived out a dream of a successful business, but also strategized so that you could have the freedom to spend much of what you accumulated during your hands-on working years. On the day that you die, your family receives a check from a life insurance company that has insured your life for all these years because your insurance decision was a *permanent* decision. Way back in your thirties or forties, your *Responsible Wealth Advisor* suggested life insurance as part of an overall strategy to protect the value of your intellectual capital. Because you understood how insurance worked, and knew that term insurance was only a temporary solution, you chose to commit to permanent insurance.

What has that permanent insurance done for you and your loved ones? If you die during your working years, it allows your family to pay off any outstanding loans and replace lost revenue. It also provides the working capital to keep the business afloat until someone can be hired to take it over and learn to operate the business or the business can be sold for a fair market value. If you die after you are no longer running the company, it might help you equalize your estate by leaving the business to one family member, while not disinheriting another. For example, if your younger son takes over the business but your older son is not interested in it, you might give the business to your younger son, while giving insurance proceeds to your older son for estate equalization purposes. Or, if your entire business inheritance will go to one person, your daughter for example, having additional money from insurance proceeds might give her time to learn your business and eventually take it over. It takes time to transition a business, and having less financial pressure is the best-case scenario. The possibilities that the proceeds provide are truly limitless. You might even want to sell your business through a charitable remainder trust and have the insurance replace the value to your estate. It is always a smoother transition, one with greater flexibility, when insurance is part of the overall equation, because the money is accessible when needed. I will discuss these scenarios more in Chapter 9.

So, if permanent insurance is a brilliant strategy that gives you options, who pays for it and how is it paid? My personal opinion is that when the insurance is on a business owner, the business should pay for it, but it should often be owned *outside* of the business. If the business owns the insurance it is a corporate asset and has different governing rules and tax implications on distribution of benefits. If the premiums need to be repaid to the business, I would rather the family make the capital contribution back to the company, or simply lend the money back to the company if need be. On the other hand, if the insurance is owned by the business, you need to be mindful of tax implications, alternative minimum tax issues and the potential of it being attacked by a creditor as a company asset.

To pay for the insurance, your advisor might suggest a Section 162 Bonus Plan, which allows the business to pay for the insurance, but requires that at the end of the year you will recognize those premiums as taxable income. Another strategy is that the business could lend you money and hold the policy as collateral known as *split-dollar*. Effectively, the business is lending you the money to pay premiums, and it will recapture those premiums upon death, or at some other time in the future. A third source of premium funding that is sometimes available is pension funding, whereby the insurance is owned inside of a pension plan. Pension dollars fund permanent life insurance for people inside the plan. The bottom line is that you, as a business owner, need to know that the resources necessary to put business life insurance in place can exist already, without requiring you to dip into your own pocket in order to make this happen. You can use your corporate checkbook or pension asset to make this strategy work.

When permanent insurance is being purchased on a key person and not an owner, I recommend that the policy is owned by or assigned to the business. Depending on your objectives, there could be many ways of determining how or when the key person would be eligible for the money inside of the policy. If you decide to put retirement money away for this person, you might set up a non-qualified plan, a deferred compensation plan or a selective retirement plan. During working years, perhaps the cash value would only be accessible to them if a disability occurred. In advance of retirement, you might structure a deferred compensation plan to pay a set sum of money each year for a given number of years, and have the policy reimburse the company upon the person's death. For example, the key person would receive $100,000 for ten years upon retirement. The sum of this is $1,000,000 of benefits, so the business owner would set up a plan with a permanent insurance policy to have either enough cash value accessible at the time of retirement or a large enough death benefit to reimburse the company for money distributed for the years prior to the key person's death. Your *Responsible Wealth Advisor* can help you set up the right type of plan with the appropriate insurance to fund that plan, but it is still important that you know some of the possibilities to strategize for your business and protect yourself simultaneously.

Funding Business Agreements

Life insurance can also be used to fund agreements such as a buy-sell, cross-purchase, and wait-and-see agreement. When more than one person's interest is at hand in ownership, each person needs to protect himself in the event that the other dies. Life insurance is purchased and the beneficiary may be the shareholder, partner, another key employee and so on, depending on the objectives. Upon the payout, the beneficiary has the capital to buy back the shares from the deceased's family at a fair market value that was predetermined by the business valuation in the agreement.

The decision to have life insurance to protect your business interests is critical, and should be an integral part of your business succession planning. Premiums are more favorable at younger ages and better health. You are not getting any younger, and typically not getting any healthier, so insurance should be established sooner rather than later. It is unfortunate to see business owners unable to fund their agreements with insurance because they are in poor health. It is a planning tool that has tremendous benefits, but it is not a luxury that everyone has.

COLI & BOLI

Individuals and small business owners are not the only ones who purchase life insurance. COLI (Corporately Owned Life Insurance), is placed on key individuals and is owned by a corporation. The insurance can be used for a variety of purposes. To name just a few, it may be a part of a deferred compensation plan as an incentive for the employee at retirement. Or, it might be a perk for the employee, in which case his family would own the death benefit, but the company would retain the cash value until retirement. Life insurance could also be used to compensate the company altogether for losing the valuable asset that they had – you. Because you are a most valuable asset, one whose intellectual capital is part of the magic behind your business, your life is worth insuring even more than any equipment you might have.

Life insurance in the private sector is often sold as aspirin for a headache – an agent gives you a headache by making you fear the impact of your premature death and then sells you life insurance to take that headache away. When purchased correctly, life insurance can be a very valuable asset class, and corporations and banks alike know this to be true. When banks purchase life insurance on their key employees, it is known as BOLI – Bank Owned Life Insurance. If you look at the financial statements of many of the public banks, as well as public or mutually owned insurance companies, you will see that life insurance as a Tier One asset. It is considered safe and secure. The best companies with the brightest accountants and attorneys know that life insurance is a fundamental component of any business. On the small business side, however, it is a challenge to get the message out there because we are inundated with counter-marketing each day in favor of passive investments like mutual funds. Financial professionals often take the path of least resistance and fail to educate their clients on life insurance. They would prefer to sell the easy investments as a retirement lottery ticket (so to speak) instead of teaching clients to invest according to the Hierarchy of Financial Assets that I talked about in Chapter 6.

Part II: Protecting Your Personal Assets as a Business Owner

Your business is often the greatest financial asset you own outside of your own abilities. No matter how you own your business – in a corporation, LLC, as a partner and so on – you still effectively own the business personally. That is, it belongs to you and it is part of the entire pool of assets that you own, such as your house or stocks in a public company. Many people spend a great deal of time protecting their business from the inside. However, they neglect to insulate themselves on the *personal* side. For example, if you get into a car accident and you are sued and you do not have adequate liability coverage, the other party will attempt to attack any asset that you own, *including your business*. You might have the best protection available for your business, but if you are not covered adequately on the personal side, you are putting everything you own at risk. The remainder of this chapter will detail many ways in which you can protect yourself and complete your overall financial plan. As always, you can work with a *Responsible Wealth Advisor* to specify the areas that pertain to you personally.

Property & Casualty Insurance

You will spend your life working hard to secure a solid financial future for yourself and your family. Much of the income you will generate will be transferred into your lifestyle in the form of two major purchases: a home and a car (probably *many* cars!). By virtue of the risks that come hand-in-hand with each of these items, *property and casualty insurance* protects us from liability from most accidents that are caused either on our properties or by our automobiles. In the event that you or your immediate family member ever lost a lawsuit due to an accident, you would always want an insurance company (not you) to write a check for damages. You would not want to risk assets being lost from your estate.

Your homeowners' insurance, auto insurance and umbrella policy (additional liability insurance above and beyond your home and auto) should be coordinated to provide the maximum possible coverage. Despite the temptation you might feel when you see how costly premiums can be, there is never a time as a business owner that you should settle for less than the maximum coverage possible. If a check ever needs to be written, you do not want to be forced to personally cover any deficit caused by insufficient insurance. You have a tremendous amount at stake if someone were to attack your assets. The perception is that business owners have deeper pockets, so in the event of a lawsuit, attorneys will look to take everything you have. You are very vulnerable if you do not take the right precautions.

A higher deductible on your homeowners' and auto insurance can help you control the costs associated with the premiums. The higher the deductible, the lower the premium. The insurance company assumes that they have less at risk when the deductible is higher because you as the customer will need to pay a larger portion if there is a claim. Typically, I see people who have deductibles of $500, when in fact they would never submit a claim for such a low amount of money. If they were to file a claim, their premiums may increase, not to mention the hassle they would incur by dealing with the claim in the first place. In reality, you can probably handle a small claim and a deductible of $1,000 to 1,500 or more. You may want to investigate the cost savings of making this adjustment.

Personal liability insurance, known commonly as an umbrella policy, is additional coverage that is above and beyond the liability limits of your homeowner's and auto insurance. These policies provide coverage of $1,000,000 or more, and the premiums are often only a few hundred dollars per year. It pays to get quotes from a few different carriers through a qualified property and casualty agent. You might even find that the money you saved by increasing your deductibles on your homeowner's and auto policies will offset the cost of an umbrella policy.

Your Future

We insure many of our possessions from liability, damage or even theft. But how do we protect our future? How do we insure ourselves? There are four ways to protect our legacies in the event of unforeseen circumstances:

- *Disability insurance* continues to provide us income if we become too sick or hurt to work.
- *Medical insurance* pays medical bills associated with illness or injury.
- *Long-term care insurance* covers us when we cannot perform the activities of daily living any longer.
- *Life insurance,* which can be the most robust insurance of all, protects our family in the event of premature death and allows us greater flexibility to spend our fortune if and when we are healthy and live long lives.

Disability Insurance

Just as we need to protect our property, we also need to protect our income. As the entrepreneur, you *are* the asset – the sole source of income and benefits – so disability income insurance becomes one of the most important financial products to implement. You and your family would want to continue to live with the same financial security if something were to happen to you and you could no longer work. You owe it to them and you owe it to yourself.

When determining which disability insurance to purchase, first read the company's definition of disability. The policy you buy should cover you under your *own occupation*, meaning that the claim will be paid if you cannot perform the duties of the occupation you hold at the time of claim. (This is distinguished from an *any occupation* definition, which states that you will only be paid if you cannot perform duties of *any* occupation.) Your disability policy should have the maximum amount of monthly indemnity possible, and it should be *non-cancellable* and *guaranteed renewable* – meaning that the insurance company cannot terminate the contract for any reason or raise your rates. The policy should also last for the maximum period possible, a lifetime *benefit period* where possible, or benefits to age sixty-five if your cash flow does not permit the cost of the lifetime benefits. You can also adjust the waiting period between the time of disability and when a claim will be paid. Typically, there is a three-, six- or twelve-month waiting period called an *elimination period*. The longer the waiting period, the less the premium will be because you are incurring more of the risk.

The Impact of a Loss

It is difficult for us to imagine being unable to work for six months, let alone many years. It is an unfortunate reality that tragedy does strike and it is better to be prepared than left to live out our days in a state of bankruptcy.

Let's say a thirty-five-year-old entrepreneur earns $100,000 per year and has a thirty- year career ahead. In the event this person is permanently disabled and cannot work, the family loses $100,000 per year for the next thirty years, not including inflation, which is a grand total of $3,000,000 of lost earnings to the family. If we do add inflation of three percent, this number feels more like $4,757,542 of lost earnings. So, this hypothetical family is almost $5,000,000 behind expectations, and we have not accounted for the medical bills and other expenses that were necessary to keep our entrepreneur comfortable during a temporary or even permanent disability.

Group Disability Insurance

You may have established a group disability insurance plan for the benefit of your employees as a part of your employee benefit package. Do not rely on this coverage as your only source of income for your needs. Every year your rates can change, and at some point it may not be cost-effective or feasible for you to continue this benefit at the company's expense. If and when you find that you no longer have group coverage for any reason, you will then need to apply for individual disability insurance. With most companies, disability insurance is one of the more difficult insurances for which to qualify. The older you are, the more expensive your base premium will be, and the more likely it is that the insurance company will add on additional premiums if your health is not perfect. And if you have any particular health issues, these will likely be excluded from the coverage altogether.

There are other substantial weaknesses of group disability insurance. Benefits are often only a percentage of your base salary, so if your base salary is low because you take your income in other forms, such as passive distributions, the coverage is not going to come close to supporting your existing lifestyle. You will also want to know the elimination period – how many months will elapse before you receive a check? Benefit periods are also typically limited in group policies so beware if your policy only provides benefits for two or five years. You might also discover that benefits will be reduced by the amount of other benefits that you receive, such as social security disability, workers' compensation, or state disability. Could there be further reduction of benefits if you have income from additional sources? Additionally, does your group disability protect you in the event that you cannot work in your existing capacity, or does it only pay if you cannot work at all? Finally, if you are the owner of the company and eventually the company ceases to exist due to your disability, you may not be able to continue a group disability plan.

Medical Insurance

When selecting your medical insurance, it is prudent to understand the different types of plans that are available in the marketplace. The nuances of each can be described in greater detail by a qualified health insurance provider; however it is always valuable to come to the table with a basic understanding of the choices. The primary purpose of medical insurance is to protect your overall financial picture in the case of a significant medical event. However, it also coordinates the care of your overall medical treatment. To maintain key employees and to provide options and flexibility, you may consider a plan which has various options that employees may choose from. Typically, the employees will pick up the costs for richer, more costly plans above some base benefit. The key is to provide choice and flexibility. It does not have to be at your expense. You may, however, consider using this as part of some performance-based compensation for key employees.

Health Maintenance Organizations (HMOs)

HMOs are networks of medical providers and medical facilities that enter into an agreement with an insurance company to treat that company's insured. Members of the HMOs have limited, if any, out-of-pocket cost for treatment, as long as they use the company's network of providers. The cost of care with an HMO is typically less than a POS or PPO and the most restrictive of the four types of plans.

Point-of-Service Plans (POS Plans)

POS Plans differentiate themselves from HMOs due to additional flexibility. There is in-network care that has the lowest potential out-of-pocket cost, and non-network care which is available for additional charges, deductibles and co-insurance. The POS Plan provides more options for members who want the ability to have more choices for their healthcare for a slightly higher cost.

Preferred Provider Organizations (PPOs)

PPOs are traditional health insurance plans that provide coverage after individuals have met their deductibles and co-insurance limits. Insureds are not limited to network physicians. This type of arrangement allows for the highest degree of flexibility for a significantly increased cost.

Consumer Driven Health Care

Consumer Driven Health Care (CDHC) is a concept that encourages the individual to take more ownership for decisions pertaining to health care. This includes the right to have a high-deductible medical insurance plan with a strategy for saving and accessing the money inside a special savings vehicle to use for the deductible if the need for treatment occurs. The premiums of a high deductible plan would be less, and if the need for health care arises, the person would pay more out-of-pocket for that care and thus use money saved in one of the savings accounts specified. Health Savings Accounts (HSAs), Health

Reimbursement Accounts (HRAs) and Flexible Savings Accounts (FSAs) are three types of accounts that are used in this scenario. Because consumers are responsible for more of the cost, they are incented to use a less costly (but equally effective) protocol, such as opting for a generic prescription over a more expensive name brand. Overall, the concept allows consumers to manage their own medical spending, while also insuring their risk in the event of large medical bills.

Long-term Care Insurance

As an employer, remember that you, your employees and members of their families are all getting older and perhaps less healthy as time goes on. Every day on NBC, Willard Scott broadcasts 100 year-old men and women on the side of the Smucker's jar. It sounds like an exciting milestone to turn 100, but old age does not come with the promise of good health. At some point, our activities of daily living might be hindered due to medical conditions. For some of us, this will occur earlier in life than we might anticipate. These activities of daily living are the triggers that spark the need for long-term care, and they include the inability to eat, bathe, dress, transfer and use the bathroom. Not everyone goes to a facility to receive the help that is needed. Some people are cared for by family members or hired healthcare workers. There are a multitude of options regarding care for a loved one, and often there is no game plan established prior to the loss of abilities. No matter how old you are, consider how you would want your care handled if you became unable to care for yourself. I have seen families torn apart over these issues because of the raw emotion, as well as the cost of care.

The cost of a facility or a private caregiver can be astronomical. Without long-term care planning and insurance you are self-insuring, which means you plan to pay for every expense out-of-pocket. Keep in mind that you and your spouse might be living off of a limited pool of assets, so it is very challenging to determine what amount of money is spent on one person's care, recognizing that the other will need money to live on or could even end up in a similar state at some point.

Some feel that Medicaid is an option – which requires the insured and spouse to be nearly without assets. Medicaid is coverage for the poor. Lest you think giving away all of your assets is a viable solution, I ask you this: Have you worked your whole life so that you can have nothing at the end?

Long-term care insurance is a relatively simple way to select the type of care you will receive during the years of care you might need. It protects the assets that will be left to your spouse, children, or charities. Ideally, you will want to purchase coverage for facility and/ or at-home care from a quality company. Care can last for many years, so researching the financial strength of the company is crucial. Long-term care insurance may be offered as an employee benefit paid for by the employee but at a discount through your company.

Life Insurance

As explained previously, life insurance is money delivered at some point in the future. In the early stages of your career as an entrepreneur, you are building your income and life insurance acts as a protection to continue an inflow of money to your family in the event you die prematurely. Otherwise, the financial impact to your family could be devastating. Buying life insurance is a financial decision where the element of love and concern for others comes into play. No other form of insurance requires you to care about someone else as much as life insurance because it will directly impact the life of someone you love.

My objective is to shed some light on what life insurance really is, and how you can effectively use it so that it may be viewed as an asset and not a liability. In an overall financial plan, life insurance acts as a non-correlated asset, as previously discussed. This better positions your financial plan for greater stability during times of economic crisis or market swings. In addition, besides paying a death benefit to your family, another very important benefit of a permanent life insurance policy is the cash value. A permanent life insurance policy is a tremendous accumulation vehicle. You never know when you will have the need or opportunity to use this money. You might experience a downturn in your business, and you might need to borrow from yourself, or you may even have a once-in-a-lifetime business opportunity and you might not be able to get a loan for the money. The possibilities are limitless.

Life insurance has gotten a bad reputation over the years, primarily due to manipulative sales techniques used by agents. It has been misrepresented as being called an investment vehicle, which is not accurate, and many agents over the years have not explained to their clients how the policy actually works. Salespeople have also been guilty of using scare tactics, such as the fear of premature death, to frighten the consumer into making a purchase. In addition, only approximately 10 percent of the salespeople entering this career will remain for five years or more, which means that your agent is likely to have disappeared from the business by the time you are prepared to ask questions of him. It's little wonder why the public has a dislike for this industry.

Let's allow ourselves to move beyond the bad experiences, and look at life insurance from a pure asset and protection point of view. If you were to die prematurely, your family and your business would lose their leader, visionary, salesperson or financial guarantee, not to mention their lifestyle and everything that they know. Reason would dictate that it makes sense to properly insure your own life. You pay for property and casualty insurance for both personal and business purposes, and you may never have a claim on those. But, one thing is certain: We will all die. There will always be a claim on life insurance, we just don't know when. No one likes to talk about death though, so many people miss the opportunity to leverage this inevitable event and achieve a better quality of life while they are living.

Before we delve into the types of insurance, we need to determine the right amount of coverage that a person needs. Allow me to draw a comparison. If you had a four-unit rental property that generated $25,000 per year of income, would you carry only enough insurance to rebuild a two-unit property if there were a fire? No! This would clearly cut your earnings in half, not to mention that you would have a year's renovation where you would not collect any rent. Then why do people make the assumption that if you are insuring breadwinners of a family that you should insure them for so much less than they are worth? There is also an economic loss to a business in the event of a key person's demise. Insurance advisors suggest that income replacement should be in the amount of the person's *human life value.* During your working years, human life value is the economic value that is equivalent to your current earning potential.

Depending on where you are in your cycle of working, your human life value is typically up to twenty times your earnings. When I hear advisors suggest that ten times earnings is enough, I personally view this as malpractice. Let me demonstrate how this could play out. If you are thirty-five years old and earn $50,000 per year, your human life value is $1,000,000 – twenty times earnings is $1,000,000 of life insurance. (The same conclusion can be made for a business to calculate lost revenue until a key person is replaced.) If something were to happen to you prematurely, your spouse would have the burden of replacing your income or changing the family's lifestyle dramatically. By receiving insurance proceeds, your spouse would put the lump sum in a conservative investment portfolio and earn a rate of return that will be similar to your current yearly earnings. So, if the account earned 5 percent, your spouse would receive $50,000 per year to replace your income. Other advisors suggest that,because the stock market has averaged 10 percent year over year, ten times your earnings would give you the same result. There is no way that a prudent advisor would ever suggest that a person risk all of their money in the market; I advise using safe, realistic rates of return. Do not be fooled – insurance proceeds do not result in a windfall to your family. Depending on the market, even a conservative investment strategy fluctuates in its rate of return. Some years there will be slightly more and other years slightly less. Over time, the family will likely invade the principal of the account to adjust for inflation, because if you were still alive, you would be earning more than $50,000 each year. Do you see why you can never have enough?

There is also confusion about what type of insurance is the right kind to buy. *Term* versus *permanent*: which one is right for me? Let's talk about term insurance for a moment. The insurance companies examine all of your medical history, and often take blood and urine from you as well. They know enough about you to determine, from an actuarial standpoint, how long you are going to live. Then, they take that information and issue insurance to you in terms of ten-, twenty- or thirty-year maximum intervals. Are you still confused about why term insurance is so cheap and getting cheaper by the year? People who qualify for life insurance will probably live long, healthy lives! The insurance company is at very little risk of giving you twenty year's worth of life insurance. In fact, most term insurance policies never result in claims – they either expire naturally or the insured stops paying premiums at some point. Term insurance is a profit center for the insurance company.

If you have the opposite type of coverage, *permanent* insurance, you will be in the best possible situation to have a multitude of benefits throughout your lifetime. Since we know that death is inevitable, it seems logical that we would want a claim to be paid eventually, especially if we are going to pay premiums for many years. I urge you to fully understand any product that you wish to acquire, and this includes understanding the different types of permanent insurance. A *variable* insurance policy ties the strength of market returns to the value of insurance, which can be a risky endeavor if the returns are poor. *Universal* life has an accumulation account with cash, dividends and/or interest earnings, and charges within the policy can, and will, change as your age increases. As expenses go up, the policy will potentially require significantly more money paid to premiums in later years. If universal life is not properly funded, it can collapse. The reason that many people opt for variable, universal and *variable universal* life insurance (a blend of the two) is that they require lower premiums than the oldest form of permanent insurance: *whole life*. Whole life insurance is a form of permanent insurance that has a level premium, cash value and a death benefit that is guaranteed and may increase over time due to interest or dividends (which fluctuate and are not guaranteed). The right advisor will guide you by explaining the nuances in greater detail and advising you which policy is best for you.

Permanent insurance should be viewed as a wealth replacement tool that may be used in the later years. If your objectives at retirement are to maximize your income and ultimately pass on your assets to your children, grandchildren or a charity, every asset you pass on is a type of insurance, in a matter of speaking. You either transfer the risk to an insurance company, or you self-insure by hoarding your assets and simply not spending them. If you self-insure and do not spend your assets because you are preserving principal, then you do not get to fully enjoy the fruits of a lifetime of labor. If you transfer the risk to the insurance company, you get to spend what you have accumulated, and also have reserves (cash value) in your permanent life insurance policy.

Proper coverage of permanent life insurance should include a waiver of premium, which is a rider that obligates the insurance company to pay your premiums in the event that you become sick or hurt, experiencing a long-term disability. Be certain that the waiver of premium selected covers the entire premium contribution period. This disability benefit should be in addition to personal disability income insurance. The benefits go on and on. Dividends and cash value can supplement your retirement income. Cash value itself is, in many states, protected from creditors, which cannot be emphasized enough in today's litigious society.

Overall, life insurance provides a multitude of benefits and an *ace-in-the-whole* for a well planned exit strategy from your other assets. No other financial product or strategy expresses love for others, while also providing you with a financial tool that can be used for building and protecting wealth at the same time.

Final Thoughts

Your plan is only as strong as its weakest link. Having only adequate personal insurance will not help you if unforeseen circumstances affect your business. Incorporating a *Responsible Wealth Advisor* into your team of professionals will help you integrate the right financial products into your portfolio.

RESPONSIBLE WEALTH SUMMARY

- *Protecting your business assets can be accomplished via the form of entity and business agreements, and through business insurances such as property and casualty, disability and life insurance. You are only as strong as your weakest link.*
- *As an entrepreneur, your business may be vulnerable to exposure in your personal life if you are not properly protected.*
- *Personal health, disability, and long-term care insurance are vital to protecting your income in the event that you become sick or hurt and can no longer work.*
- *Personal, permanent life insurance holds a myriad of benefits, ranging from income replacement upon your demise, to helping you maximize your assets upon retirement.*

CHALLENGING THOUGHTS

- *Have you been properly advised by an attorney and/or accountant regarding the form of entity of your business?*
- *Do you have a business agreement that clearly defines what will transpire in the event of a death, disability, lawsuit, or business transfer of any kind?*
- *Has your Responsible Wealth Advisor reviewed your personal insurance policies to determine if adequate coverage and liability limits are present for your protection?*

Chapter 9
Business Succession Planning

Choose It or Lose It

Business owners review their financial statements quite frequently. We all play a mental game with ourselves in which we value our business and other assets and determine at what point we can cash out to live comfortably for the rest of our lives. This does not have to be at retirement – that day might arrive earlier than that. As entrepreneurs, we all have our own mental "walk-away number" so that if an offer were presented to buy us out, we know what that number would need to be. Our walk-away number would be the amount of money that we feel would fairly compensate us for the energy and capital that we have invested, and would be the amount of money that we could comfortably live on going forward. The conversation in our heads goes something like this: "If I can get $1,000,000 net of taxes, and invest that money at a five percent rate of return, I can have $50,000 per year without doing anything." Next, we ask ourselves if that dollar amount would provide us with the money and security that we would want to potentially live with for the rest of our lives. Did we accomplish what we set out to accomplish? Are we ready to have our time to ourselves again? If we have used the strategies of a *Responsible Wealth Advisor*, perhaps we are able to spend even more of that lump sum than just to live on interest only. Principle and interest on $1,000,000 may feel more like $80,000 per year.

Before you can ever even think about cashing in your chips and walking away from the table, there are stages of planning that need to occur. Primarily, this includes creating a value for your business that someone may ultimately purchase from you. The entity that purchases your business might not even be an outside party – it might be your own family or your key employees. Business succession includes creating a plan that is active today, and that prepares your business for any opportunity or circumstance that might occur – a purchase being only one of those circumstances. For example, you could become disabled or die prematurely. These are not the events we sit around dreaming about, but unfortunately they can and do happen to people. In a clear mind, you would never want your business to fold if you were not around to manage it, so it is imperative that you put together a safe action plan if the unexpected were to occur. Other events are not so unexpected, but still require proper planning, such as retirement of you or other key members of your organization. It is my hope for you that you recognize how foolish it would be to simply pack your bags and close the door at your retirement. But for the business to continue after you, it needs to have value *beyond* you, otherwise it is worthless to someone else under any of these circumstances.

Personally, I want my business and legacy to carry on. The best way to ensure that this will happen in the manner I choose is by writing a formal business succession plan. Admittedly, no matter how thorough the planning, if the owner retires, dies or becomes disabled, there is naturally a void that occurs. Some clients might decide to take their business elsewhere because they were loyal to you, not your company. There will always be some degree of fallout and the competition might be waiting in the wings to prey on the opportunity. Despite this, it is essential to build the value in your business as we have talked about extensively throughout this book, and also to have a business succession plan prepared in advance so that you and your family can reap the rewards of a lifetime of ingenuity.

If you are procrastinating on your business succession plan, let me remind you that time is not unlimited. There is a country song by Kenny Chesney called *Don't Blink*. The song is about an interview of an old man turning one-hundred-two years old, and he is asked about the secret to life. He says, "…when your hourglass runs out of sand, you can't flip it over and start again. Trust me friend, a hundred years goes faster than you think. So don't blink." None of us knows how much time we have to be healthy or to be here. So much planning is neglected and excused away because we get busy with other things and we see time as endless, giving us no sense of urgency. You can probably think of your own life and how time seems to be going faster and faster the older you get. If we don't plan for the things that are important, we could create a much more difficult situation for us or our loved ones down the road. Decisions made under duress are typically poor decisions. Do not let your life's work fall apart the day you disappear from your company. In a perfect world, what would you want to transpire in your absence? Would you want to retain ownership, sell the business, or pass it on to your family? Think in terms of *Responsible Wealth:* How do you want to *responsibly* handle your wealth? If you made it to the Super Bowl, the last thing you would want to do is fumble the ball in the last play to lose the game.

The first step in business succession planning is giving careful thought to your ideal scenario. Who would you want to take over your business? How would you like to see the transition go? If you are concerned about leaving the business to one child and disinheriting another, there are ways to equalize your estate. Another concern I hear from my business owner clients is the perception that if you plan for succession, you will suffer from enormous professional fees incurred in developing a plan. Translation: If the cost is high, you will realize less current cash flow and less current quality of life. The reality is that, with good planning, it may be possible to accomplish your objectives with minimal or no cost, so before worrying about the cost, decide what you would like to see unfold as a best-case scenario. A *Responsible Wealth Advisor* will help you get as close to your perfect scenario as possible. Solid business succession planning will help you live out your dreams for the business after you are gone, and a thorough plan attempts to leave no stone unturned. The relief and mental clarity of having the plan in place frees up space in your mind from worry, and leaves room for your energy to be refocused on more important areas. If that is not reason enough, the statistics show that, without a plan, your business is likely to fold rather quickly. It would be a tragedy to let a lifetime of work crumble.

Business Valuation

After you decide how you would want your business transition to progress after you leave the company, the next step in business succession planning is to determine the monetary value of your business. If you are going to invest years of your life in an entity, how do you really determine the value of what you create? How do you assess how you are doing and what you have built? When I assess a public company, I look at earnings per share and net earnings (after expenses) tell me how profitable the company is. Your scenario is probably not that cut and dry. Bear in mind, even if you are not looking to sell your company today, you always need to move forward with the perspective that you will sell it at some point and that it needs to have value. If the business is not profitable overall, you may simply own a job. Some of my associates ask me why I choose to run an agency of advisors when I could probably make more money concentrating on my personal practice and working with clients. The answer is simple. I am in the business to build something that has value and is transferrable. The alternative would be that I work solely with my own clients, and the business stops with me. In my opinion, there is also tremendous stewardship in running my firm, and I am pleased that it has value beyond me and my good name. It's not about me, it's about *we*.

Start determining your business's value by looking at your earnings and your sales. If sales continue to increase but earnings are flat, that may be a sign that your business is in trouble. This could also indicate that you have been reinvesting your earnings to help the company grow, but if you continue to do more and more business without an increase in earnings, you may have a problem on your hands. Your products might not be priced accordingly, or your process may be inefficient. I once saw a power company lose more money the more electricity the public needed. It was unable to raise its rates and lost money on each unit. As demand increased, earnings decreased dramatically. These are indicators that you need to reevaluate your price, costs or processes. In addition to keeping a watchful eye on earnings and sales, always have new opportunities and new obstacles on your radar. For example, if I owned an accounting firm, I would be mindful that tax returns are being shipped overseas in many companies. The direct result of that is that 1040s are now being commoditized due to the cheap price of foreign labor. I would project the effect that this could have on my business, and I would choose to shift the focus of my business to consulting with clients, rather than preparation of the returns themselves.

In my financial service practice, we sell health insurance. I realize that the cost of insurance continues to increase dramatically each year, and I believe at some point the federal government will be forced to step in to address this problem. Businesses cannot continue to sustain 15 to 20 percent increases each year. If and when the government puts a new healthcare system in place, the business will become commoditized and we will lose a substantial portion of our revenue from this line of business. Despite this impending situation, I believe that offering health insurance to my clients is a needed service. I will not make any long-term plans based on this revenue. No matter what, however, I will continue to use this avenue of business as a source of introduction to new clients, then approach them with the other services my firm has to offer.

When we look at a company to determine its value, we first look at earnings per share. Next we analyze the sales figures. Then we move to the uniqueness of a business. What is your unique ability as an organization? What makes you different, and is there value in that? If you are not unique to the marketplace, you need to give outstanding service; otherwise people are probably not doing much business with you. Sooner or later, if being the cheapest is your only strategy, you will lose on price. Look at the oil crisis we have right now. Alternative forms of energy exist, and as the cost of oil rises to excessive heights, people will begin to seek out these other forms more and more. And when the price to pump it ourselves becomes less than the cost to buy it elsewhere, we will begin to pump our own because we have plenty of oil within the U.S.

Sometimes, the value lies in your name or your unique process, which is referred to as intellectual property. Once Donald Trump or Tiger Woods endorses a product or puts his name on something, it has value. People are already waiting in anticipation for the golf course Tiger Woods has underway in Asheville, North Carolina. At other times, the value lies in other forms of intellectual capital. Management and people are the keys to success within any business. If I build an entire business around myself, and without me in the picture my business is dead, then my business has no value. My personal value is non-transferrable. When Tiger Woods endorses a product, he impacts consumers by selling his name, which in turn creates value for businesses. This is a form of intellectual capital; however, in Tiger's case, it is non-transferrable. When I talk about creating an experience and developing a process, this is where the real value of a business lies.

If the business still functions without you and/or your key people, it has value. When it is all about you, your business may accomplish certain elements that you want for your life (freedom, lifestyle), but it does not make a sellable entity. In that scenario, you would need to continue to work in order to continue to earn money. A successful business will run and earn money whether you are there or not.

Some professionals will start their careers, given trades or professions, then expand their horizons by building businesses around their work. Years ago, I had Lasik eye surgery. The doctor who performed the surgery had a surgery center where he performed twenty surgeries per day. At $4,300 per surgery, that's $86,000 a day! But what impressed me even more was the center itself and how efficiently it operated. This process is what allowed the doctor to do his work. When I arrived, the woman at the desk guided me through the paperwork. Next, I had my eye exam with another staff member, then had some tests performed. After I was prepped and ready to have my procedure, the doctor came in the room. He was cordial and we had a brief conversation; then he went right to work with the laser. When all was successfully completed, other assistants brought me back to the waiting room to book my follow-up appointment and explain my medications. The experience was incredibly professional. I never saw him again until my follow-up visit, where he again performed only the duties that he specialized in.

If you are not sure where to begin with your business valuation, a good accountant can help identify value. The number may be based on a multiple of earnings, in which every industry will have a different norm. Your accountant can also help you identify the highest and best use of the business assets. If your business owns the real estate on which it operates, it is possible that the land or building alone might be worth more than your business. The value may be in the combination of business and assets. Sometimes the sum of the parts can be worth more than the whole.

Writing the Business Succession Plan

If you have a business at this time that would have little value without you in the picture, now is the time to start changing your model or preparing your finances so that you and your estate can receive fair value for your life's work. You might cross-train a young associate or a family member to take over the business and buy you out, or you may incorporate life insurance into your plan to leave money to your heirs or a charity. Assuming you have a monetary value to your business, you have basically three exit strategies – you can retain all or some ownership, sell the business altogether or pass it on to your heirs.

Upon retirement, you might choose to retain ownership in the company. You can remain a shareholder in order to continue to earn money each year. If you retain the business in your estate and you die or become incapable of making a decision as it pertains to your ownership, your family will need to determine the next step. The biggest risk to this plan is that your family may not be in as good a position to negotiate a sale without you. You know your business, you understand its value and you know best how a transfer should be handled.

An alternative to keeping ownership would be to sell the business outright upon your retirement or have a sale triggered upon death or disability. There may be a wide market of buyers – some you might not have ever considered. The company might be sold to family members, employees, strangers or competitors. If you choose to sell to a family member, be certain to write a clear buy-sell agreement so that there are no hard feelings among other family members. Financing can be accomplished through any of the Raising Capital strategies noted in Chapter 7.

Selling your business to your employees can be accomplished directly or through an ESOP, an Employee Stock Ownership Plan. In this arrangement, your employees can receive stock options, buy stock directly, be granted stock as a bonus or obtain stock through their profit sharing plan. Here in New Jersey, there was an engineering firm that implemented an ESOP as part of a strategy to sell the firm from the larger shareholders to other employees of the firm, so that the founders could ultimately get the cash out of their firm. A few of the partners happened to be my clients. Through the use of the ESOP, the company was able to make tax deductible contributions to the retirement plans of the employees by utilizing company stock that was being valued each year. In addition, they had a stock option plan in place which enabled employees of the firm to also purchase stock outside of the ESOP. Eventually, the company merged with another firm that cashed out all of the existing stock that was owned by the employees.

Another client who is in the printing business had been considering a merger or sale to a competitor. He used this friendly competitor as a wholesaler to complete some larger jobs that his company was not equipped to handle. The company liked his client base and could fill all of their printing needs, so there was a fit on all sides. This other company was, however, larger than his company. Keep in mind that if you merge with another larger company, it is usually more of an acquisition than a merger, which leaves you in the position of lesser power. An alternative for my client could be to instead choose to sell to private money investors or a hedge fund, or to sell directly to the public via an IPO (initial public offering) and eventually stock. If the company has strong earnings and a strong business model, the return will be greater. Identifying potential buyers early is always helpful.

Your last and most common exit strategy would be to pass the business on to someone, typically one or more of your children or a key employee. If you decide to go this route, I would encourage you to leave plenty of what I like to call "mistake money." This would be the financial cushion that would allow your successor to get up and running without strict financial pressure, otherwise there would be little room for trial and error. To equalize the inheritance you would give to one child over another if one receives the business, many estate plans use life insurance. One child will get the business, and the other(s) will receive other assets or insurance proceeds. Be sure that you do not create a disadvantage to the child receiving the business – he/she is receiving the value of the company, but is also doing a job to earn income and keep the business running. You would not want to give the others cash and leave one with only a job and responsibility.

Charitable Remainder Trusts

For the business owner with charitable intent, a *charitable remainder trust* (CRT) may be an ideal scenario for business transfer. A CRT allows you to gift an appreciated asset (such as a business) to a trust, which is ultimately sold tax-free. The proceeds from the sale of the business provide income in the form of annuity payments. Prior to the sale, the shares are gifted to a charitable remainder trust, and you (the business owner) are the income beneficiary of the trust. Let's use me as the example to show you how this would work. Long before I chose to exit or sell my business, I would gift all of the shares of my business to the charitable remainder trust that my attorney has designed and drafted (of which I would be the income beneficiary). Based on the total value of the trust (which would be the present value of the future gift of my business), two calculations are completed. (1) How much income will I draw from the trust when I intend to retire? This amount can be based on a fixed or variable interest rate. (2) How much will likely remain in the trust to be donated upon my death? The older I am, the greater the present value of the future gift will be because there is likely to be more money remaining in the trust to be donated. This present value of the future gift creates a significant tax deduction for the grantor.

Because I am in control, I will decide when the business is sold by the trust. It can be sold to key employees, another entity and so on. When this occurs, the trust receives the proceeds, and I begin to draw my income stream from the trust. The money I receive comes to me as investment income, and I can choose my stream of income to be subject to a fixed or variable interest rate. Depending on whether I was advised to have a charitable remainder annuity trust (CRAT) or a charitable remainder unitrust (CRUT) and how the investments are structured inside of that trust, I receive income for the rest of my life. Upon my demise, the money remaining in the trust would be left to a charity. In order for my family to still receive as close to the full value from my business as possible when I die, I would have also coordinated the decision to use life insurance in conjunction with creating the trust. Life insurance is a powerful part of this strategy because it replaces the money that your family would have otherwise received from the sale. If necessary, my team of advisors would have guided me regarding an irrevocable life insurance trust (ILIT) if those proceeds needed to be free of estate tax.

From a tax perspective, charitable remainder trusts can be a planning strategy because they may allow a business to be sold free of capital gains tax. If the business has little or no basis, this strategy allows for an even greater amount of the proceeds to be kept intact. Instead of selling a business outright for say $1,000,000 and ending up with net proceeds of $700,000, you would have the full $1,000,000 in the trust. You would have use of the full amount to generate income for the rest of your life.

Charitable remainder trusts are very complex financial tools that require the advice of a qualified attorney and accountant to work in conjunction with your *Responsible Wealth Advisor* to assist you in implementing this type of strategy. Your team might be able to create a financial macroeconomic plan that can show you how to get money out of other tax sheltered vehicles as well.

Funding the Business Succession Plan

Your business succession plan can be funded or unfunded. Funding the plan means putting the right provisions in place to execute the plan. If you are going to sell the business, did you make sure that the business is bankable? And if it is not, are you prepared to hold the note in an installment sale or have the paperwork drawn up to have a private annuity paid to you from the sale? Has your plan specifically identified what assets will be sold with the business? Were the assets divided appropriately?

I believe that you should always transfer the financial risk of death or disability to an insurance company, and there are a variety of ways to fund the insurance as discussed in Chapter 8.

As business owners, we look at our financial statements and decide, based on our net worth, if we have enough to live comfortably for the rest of our lives. There is a certain amount of financial freedom in knowing that you can walk away. Young business owners project into the future and dream of living off the fruits of their labor, and that dream helps to propel them forward and stay focused on the plan. Overall, most entrepreneurs continue to look for new opportunities, even when they have sold their main investment, because it is innate for them to recognize that good investments are all around. Some retire only to build other businesses, and still others retire and work with charities, donating their knowledge to those who need help. One of my mentors, Tim, who also was a general agent in the insurance industry, retired and went on to be founder of a lay Catholic leadership training program, and even recently wrote a book called *Good Leaders, Good Shepherds*. Entrepreneurs who really understand purpose and value have a difficult time retiring in the traditional sense. They have so much knowledge that they either continue to teach the next generation what they have done, or they take their wisdom and apply it to a new venture. I believe sharing is what it's all about. Business succession planning is not about the game being over. It is merely about transitioning your business in the most effective, longstanding way possible. Your hard work should live beyond you.

RESPONSIBLE WEALTH SUMMARY

- *For your business to succeed after you are gone, it needs to have value beyond you.*
- *The cost of not having a business succession plan can be devastating to your business and personal wealth. A Responsible Wealth Advisor can show you strategies to minimize the fees associated with professionals who will help you implement the plan.*
- *Business succession planning involves preparation for the many circumstances that can cause a business transition from you to another party – a sale, your retirement, death, or disability, to name a few.*

CHALLENGING THOUGHTS

- *What measures have you put in place to build your business in such a way that it will survive, even without you at the helm?*
- *Have your advisors encouraged you to consider the perfect scenario of how you would like your business to continue after you are gone, and helped you execute a business succession plan to make sure that happens?*
- *What financial provisions have you put in place to formulate a smooth transition from you to another party? Is the business bankable? Is there cash or cash flow to run the business?*

Chapter 10

Planning Your Estate

Protect Your Life's Work

Some people think that writing a will is a bad omen. Little do they know if something were to happen to them there is no travesty worse than dying without the proper documentation in place. Have you ever known a husband to be forced to go to probate court when his wife died with no will because her car was only listed in her name? This is only a minor example of the harsh realities that people find themselves facing. Ironically, when it comes to planning your estate, you have a plan whether you have taken the time to write one or not. It is either the plan you have chosen by establishing the proper documents, or it is your state's intestate laws that specify the distribution formula and appointments the state will use if you die without estate management documentation. Wouldn't you rather your assets be transferred on your terms and not the government's?

Given how states manage money and benefits, I suggest you execute your own plan, not theirs. All of your planning – business succession planning as well as personal estate planning – needs to coordinate together. Do not be fooled – if you only complete half of the process by drafting either the business succession documents or the estate documents, you could be creating just as big a problem for yourself as not doing anything at all. You could potentially leave either your business or your family in dire straights...or both. For example, many business owners choose to leave their business to one or more children and leave life insurance or another asset to the other children for the purposes of equalizing the inheritance. If one document has been completed and the other has not, one child might profit from a windfall and another might be completely omitted from receiving an inheritance. Another potential mishap could occur if you leave a business to children, but neglect to provide a continuing income stream to your spouse. Let's say that the business's success determines your spouse's income, and your child is ill-prepared to run your business and does not succeed. What then? This ties into yet another problem that I have seen replicated, which is the potential that there is no liquid asset left behind. With no cash on hand, there is no way to buy a child the time to learn your business, to pay inheritance taxes or to support the many other capital needs that arise upon a death. This can lead to a forced sale of an asset that was not your intention, and not the desire of your heir.

Walk yourself through an exercise of your own documents: What would happen if you died tomorrow? What would transpire, both on the side of your estate and with your business? Overall, the process of estate planning will require expertise from an attorney, an accountant, and your *Responsible Wealth Advisor* to ensure a thorough plan is written and executed the way that you choose. Business owners and entrepreneurs need to give special consideration to the establishment and implementation of a business succession plan that is coordinated with your personal estate planning. We have discussed this at great length in Chapter 9, and I encourage you to work with your advisors on all aspects of your planning to ensure that they are working in conjunction with one another. You have worked hard to earn and acquire your total estate, and all of the pieces should be put in place regarding how you personally choose to distribute those holdings upon your demise.

Start With a Will

Assets pass at death by means of ownership and beneficiary arrangements. Estate documents are referred to as *wills* and *trusts*. Documents, ownership and beneficiary arrangements need coordination to properly plan your estate. Keep in mind that, as you grow and build your assets, a variety of tools and techniques are available to assist you, both in achieving your objectives and in minimizing your taxes.

A basic estate plan starts with a *will* that specifies details regarding the management of your assets, as well as appointment of guardianship for your minor children. Asset management upon your demise may be accomplished through the use of trusts established for the benefit of loved ones and charities. Trusts are entities that own assets for the benefit of its beneficiaries. Trust documents provide instruction and direction on how you have planned for your assets to be distributed for the benefit of your beneficiaries, as well as carrying out your intentions regarding the management of your assets. If you have a substantial estate comprised of everything you own including your life insurance, a properly structured will may also minimize any potential estate taxes. This can be accomplished through a *testamentary trust*, also known as a *credit shelter* or *bypass trust,* which allows use of the tax-free exemptions enabling passage of your assets *tax free* to your beneficiaries.

In addition to trusts managing assets upon your demise, they may also own and manage assets while you are alive. There are two forms of trusts: a revocable trust, which may be changed or altered throughout your lifetime, and an irrevocable trust, which may not be changed or altered throughout your lifetime. Trusts can contain many different types of assets. The most common asset inside of an *irrevocable trust*, for example, is life insurance, which is set up to avoid adding the proceeds of the insurance to your estate. When proceeds are added to your estate, this potentially increases your state and/or federal tax liability thus reducing the assets ultimately left to your heirs. This trust is funded through irrevocable gifts that you make throughout your lifetime, which are used to pay the insurance premiums, and they cannot be rescinded. The downside of this type of trust, however, is that the benefits that you may have personally enjoyed throughout your lifetime will be eliminated or restricted.

An additional standard document for estate planning is a *power of attorney*, which enables the selection of someone to manage your assets and to handle financial affairs for you in the event you are unable or incapable of doing so while you are alive. The last document is a *living will*, or advanced directive. This document enables you to indicate the extent of treatment you wish to receive in the event you cannot represent yourself. It will dictate how far you want doctors to go to keep you alive in the event that you require life support or emergency medical treatment.

Finally, as it relates to your estate, the use of Family Limited Partnerships, Limited Liability Companies, and other forms of legal entities may provide estate and income tax savings. In general, these entities must be established for a business purpose. The ownership of assets such as real estate, business interest and investments are typically acceptable for this purpose. These entities provide you with the ability to maintain control of the assets, while enabling estate tax reduction through current gifts of partnership interest. Discounting of asset values may also be possible due to lack of liquidity and marketability. By gifting interest in these entities, you are reducing your estate by the current gift's value, along with the future appreciation of that gift. Income shifting opportunities may also be available through distributions from the entity. These different forms of entities may also provide an added layer of asset protection planning, especially in relation to lawsuits and judgments. Although a very complex topic, professionals in this field of law can assist you in selecting appropriate strategies for asset ownership and protection that depend upon your objectives and personal situation.

RESPONSIBLE WEALTH SUMMARY

- *When it comes to planning your estate, you have a plan whether you have taken the time to write one or not. It is either the plan you have chosen by establishing the proper documents, or it is your state's intestate laws that will prevail.*

- *Working with your Responsible Wealth Advisor, as well as your attorney and accountant, you can create your will, trusts, living will, and powers of attorney so that your wishes are executed in the event you are not able to execute them.*

CHALLENGING THOUGHTS

- *What would happen if you died tomorrow? What would transpire, both on the side of your estate and with your business? Do you even know?*

- *Have you had direct conversations with your family to discuss your wishes in the event of your death? Does your family know where the documentation is, or how to get in touch with your attorney or advisors?*

Chapter 11

Leaving a Legacy

The Ripple Effect of Your Life

"What you leave behind is not what is engraved in stone monuments, but what is woven into the lives of others."

— Pericles

The lesson I impart to my colleagues and clients every day is this: Be conscious and aware of how you are living your life, because time is not in endless supply. Although my parents never worked for themselves, the wisdom they passed on has given me several gifts that helped me to get to where I am today. I came away from my childhood understanding that the time to embrace life is today, because tomorrow doesn't wait for you to catch up. *This is part of their legacy*, and I am proud to have shared it with you.

Early in my life, I never thought about what my legacy would be. I was determined to work for myself and get ahead for primarily financial reasons, even though I did not quite have a game plan for what line of business to pursue. I just knew that I also wanted to be in control of my own destiny, and perhaps you want to be in control of your life also. Many of us have similar stories that get us to the point of taking a step and moving from the norm to the world of what some call *risk*. I prefer to refer to it as the world of *opportunity* and *possibility*. Wherever you are on your journey, whether it is the beginning, end or somewhere in the middle of your life, we all have opportunities to grow and reach that next level. As they say, America is the land of opportunity!

Are these some of the ideas that cross your mind? *I can do that! I can be my own boss. I can own my company. I can build something bigger than I already have created! I can make a difference.* If you haven't reached that point yet, what's holding you back? For some of us, it begins at a young age, and for others the vision of what is possible does not appear until much later, if ever.

My objective in this book was to help you build and protect your life's work while building a life of *Responsible Wealth*. It is my wish that you not only improve your top and bottom lines, but also maintain a balanced life. If you spend twenty-four/seven on your business and there is nothing else left, you have not truly succeeded. You might be in jeopardy of leaving this earth with a substantially different legacy than what you intended. Real success is building a life of *Responsible Wealth*, not just *financial gain*.

At the End of the Day, It's All About the People

How will people remember you when you are gone? On some level, we all ponder this question. Some of us are smart enough to recognize that the things we are doing at this very moment will dictate this answer. How we behave *right now* will affect how others see us long after we are not around. "Legacy" is not about leaving money behind in an endowment, although that is a wonderful and generous thing to do. A client passed away several months ago, and I was not privy to all of his charitable donations. Imagine my surprise when I attended a function at a rabbinical college near his home, and I saw his name on the main building. I had no idea that he had been so involved with the institution. Overall, our legacy is in our name and the long-term impact that we have on the lives and families of others, not in our bragging rights. No matter what form your donation takes, you have the potential to greatly impact the lives of others each and every day. Treat people right and stand for integrity, because the ripple effect goes farther than you can measure.

In the course of a day, most of us work eight hours, sleep eight hours, and are living our lives for eight hours. If you eliminate the sleep time, you are most likely spending half of your life at work. If you are a business owner, you control that environment because you are in the leadership role. When that environment is based on integrity and doing the right thing for others, you influence the lives of those who work for you. You have the opportunity to serve as a mentor, parental figure, friend, colleague, and teacher. I have even been a marital counselor at times. If others trust you and value your advice, this is the manifestation of your legacy. In other words, your legacy is not thirty years away – it's now. You are a part of people's lives, and you will be faced with the chance to help people through the hard times and celebrate with them in the good times. Standing side-by-side with others in life is one of the ways in which people will remember you. Making a difference in the lives of others is not part of a job description. If people look up to you and you can be a positive influence in their lives, you will have done a great thing for them, one with a lasting impact. This is what creating a legacy is all about.

I often think of our politicians who are either revered or disgraced during their tenures. At times, the entire world is subject to their moments of leadership, and at other times their antics or failures. To this day, when I hear the name Bill Clinton I think of Monica Lewinsky. Lucky for him, there was some time after the scandal and before he left office for people to forget what happened a bit. And George W? I think of a war that we cannot seem to find our way out of, an economy that's in shambles and a housing market that is falling apart. Even if none of that was his fault, this is still his legacy. These are the thoughts that are conjured up when his name is spoken.

When you are in charge, people are watching you all the time. They are watching when you are helping others, dealing with clients or holding a meeting. They are also watching you when you are slacking off, being disrespectful to others or unprepared for a client meeting. Returning phone calls the same day is imperative. If you do not have the information that a client is looking for, call and tell them that so they are not waiting for the phone to ring. If you are not doing the right thing right now, don't apologize for it. Start doing the right thing now. It really is never too late to turn your reputation around. Let people know that you care in the little ways, not just the big glorious moments.

After learning the news that he had the disease ALS, Lou Gehrig said in his farewell speech, "Fans, for the past two weeks you have been reading about the bad break I got. Yet today, I consider myself the luckiest man on the face of this earth. I have been in ballparks for seventeen years and have never received anything but kindness and encouragement from you fans." Lou Gehrig appreciated the life he had been given, and influenced the lives of others. And more recently, Randy Pausch, the professor from Carnegie Mellon whose Last Lecture launched him into fame, has taught people around the world to live for today. He did not create that message upon news of his terminal cancer. He had been living that way, inspiring others for years. These are the famous examples of living your legacy. You do not, however, have to be famous to have a truly significant impact on others each and every day.

Responsible Wealth is about taking responsibility for what you stand for and what you represent. A career as an entrepreneur could span a lifetime, and the number of lives you touch is impossible to count. Every time you say hello to a person walking down the street who recognizes you, every time you care enough to ask a waitress her name, each time that you hand someone your business card...these are the little interactions of life that are building your reputation one block at a time. You may have heard the Starfish Story, by Loren Eisley. A young boy was standing among a sea of starfish stranded on the beach. A man who was walking by asked the boy why he bothered to throw the starfish back into the ocean, one at a time, when there were hundreds that would die. His perception was that the boy could not make a difference, and the boy smiled at him and said "I made a difference for that one."

You too can make a difference in the lives of one or many that you touch. Your book has not yet been written. I encourage you to make the world your starfish and start building a legacy right now and embrace the gift of leadership you have been given as an entrepreneur. You have no way of knowing when your hourglass will run out of sand. The time to accept the gifts you have been given is now. Protect them so that they live on long after you.

RESPONSIBLE WEALTH SUMMARY

- *Your legacy is occurring right now. It is not an event in the future.*
- *You have an impact on each person and each event that you encounter. Responsible Wealth is about leaving the situation better than the way you found it.*

CHALLENGING THOUGHTS

- *Are you embracing your entrepreneurial world of unlimited possibility? Are you present to the fact that opportunity is around you? In what ways are you taking advantage of all that you have available to you?*
- *Write your eulogy today. What would you say to people, and what would you want people to say about you?*